Wendy Bowles is Senior Lecturer in Social Work at Charles Sturt University and co-author of *Research for Social Workers* (Allen & Unwin/ Routledge). She has served on the National Ethics Committee of the Australian Association of Social Workers.

Michael Collingridge is Professor and Head of the School of Humanities and Social Sciences at Charles Sturt University, and has taught and researched in professional ethics and law for many years.

Steven Curry is Research Fellow at the Centre for Applied Philosophy and Public Ethics, University of Melbourne, and has worked with government and professional organisations on issues of ethics and professional practice.

Bruce Valentine is Lecturer in Social Work at Charles Sturt University and has extensive experience in the fields of health and welfare.

D1434172

Ethical practice in social work

AN APPLIED APPROACH

Wendy Bowles
Michael Collingridge
Steven Curry
Bruce Valentine

Open University Press

Open University Press
McGraw-Hill Education
McGraw-Hill House
Shoppenhangers Road
Maidenhead
Berkshire
England
SL6 2QL

email: enquiries@openup.co.uk
world wide web: www.openup.co.uk

and Two Penn Plaza, New York, NY 10121-2289, USA

First published in Australia and New Zealand in 2006 by Allen & Unwin Pty Ltd

A catalogue record of this book is available from the British Library

ISBN-10: 0 335 2220 3 X (pb) 0 335 22204 8 (hb)
ISBN-13: 9780 335 222049 (hb) 9780 335 222032 (pb)

Library of Congress Cataloging-in-Publication Data
CIP data applied for

Set in 11/14 pt ACaslon by Midland Typesetters, Australia
Printed by South Wind Production, Singapore

10 9 8 7 6 5 4 3 2 1

Contents

Preface

This book started out as a conversation between two of us (Wendy Bowles and Michael Collingridge). A new way of thinking about ethical social work practice was emerging from our teaching at Charles Sturt University and the workshops we conducted with practitioners in different organisations and several countries. Initially referred to as 'power ethics', we later abandoned this term in favour of a more applied approach but we retained our central argument that being ethically articulate empowers practitioners. At Charles Sturt we are fortunate in being able to teach professional ethics as an exchange, and sometimes an argument, between philosophers and practitioners/academics. Many of the philosophers who have taught with us in ethics also work in the university's Centre for Applied Philosophy and Public Ethics in Canberra.

Our social work ethics classes have been enlivened by three of the authors (Wendy, Michael and Steve Curry) working through their ideas with the social work students, many of whom bring with them a wealth of practice and life experience. The fourth author (Bruce Valentine), became involved in the project firstly as a PhD student researching social justice, then as an academic. He brings a lifetime of professional practice and management experience in the human services. As a student text, we had in mind that it might be used by social work students and their lecturers in the later part of their social work programs when the students have some understanding of the nature of social work and social work practice.

This book is a conversation between four different voices from three different professions: social work, law and philosophy. Each of us have different styles and idiosyncrasies. The book represents our collective view about the power of ethics in professional life.

Though each chapter usually had a primary author, we all contributed to, worried over and edited each one and thus we all share the responsibility for what you are about to read. Thinking back on the process of writing the book we realise that we applied the themes we advocate. The book also illustrates the strength of four very different perspectives working together—an example of our argument for a pluralist approach to ethical practice. We remain good friends and colleagues.

Acknowledgments

Too many people have contributed to this book for all to be acknowledged individually. The case studies represent an amalgam of stories, anecdotes, experiences and even jokes that we began collecting many years ago. Some social workers offered cases and asked that they be disguised to protect the parties involved, while others contributed through their previously published accounts, which we have acknowledged in the text. To all those people who wittingly and unwittingly contributed, we express our thanks.

Professor Seumas Miller, Director of the Centre for Applied Philosophy and Public Ethics, encouraged us to write this book and cracked the whip. Others we'd like to thank include Bill Anscombe, Marianne Bush, Professor Richard Hugman and our colleagues and students in the School of Humanities and Social Sciences—they all helped us formulate our ideas over the years.

Thanks also to Lesley Chenoweth and Donna McAuliffe for permission to reproduce the diagram of 'An inclusive model of ethical decision making' that we discuss in chapter 9, as well as our anonymous reviewers who helped us to sharpen our arguments and made global suggestions. We didn't always agree with them but are still most grateful for their contribution to the final version of this book. *Australian Social Work* gave permission to adapt large parts of an article (Collingridge, Miller and Bowles 2001), previously published in that journal, in our chapter 7.

Finally a special thanks to Professor Jan Fook, the series editor, Elizabeth Weiss, our publisher, and Alexandra Nahlous, our editor at

Allen & Unwin, for their patience and detailed advice. Ethical practice in social work requires practitioners to take an ethical position including accepting responsibility for their practice. As authors, all errors are ours.

Every effort has been made to contact the copyright holders of material used. Please contact the publisher directly for any copyright enquiries.

Introduction

Ethics is an integral part of the working life of every social and other human service worker. Making decisions in situations where there is no simple right or wrong solution, working between people and organisations, advocating for those who cannot advocate for themselves, having to justify your actions to people who are questioning why something was done or not done—these are just some of the daily challenges social workers encounter. Faced with complex situations and conflicting interests, and arguing for different courses of action, social workers need a solid base of ethical understanding and decision-making ability if they are to make a difference to other people's lives, and personally thrive in their own jobs.

In this book we argue that not only is ethics fundamental to social work, it is a source of empowerment for social workers. Many people, social workers in particular, feel uneasy about terms such as 'power' and 'empowerment' being associated with ethics. Power, especially unchecked power, is usually associated with being unethical. We think of dictators doing terrible things to people, or faceless bureaucrats making unethical decisions, hidden away from anyone who could hold them accountable for their actions. Social work itself has had some bad moments in its history when it has acted as a tool of the state to oppress disadvantaged groups. Images of social workers removing babies without good reason, or abusing their power in other ways, are all too familiar. Power has always had a contradictory place in the social work profession. Radical social workers of the 1970s and more recently the critical approaches since the mid-1990s have called on social workers to confront issues of power. But how?

Ethics lies at the heart of social work practice. Ethics itself is a source of power. In an increasingly hostile world, power can certainly be used for unethical purposes but, in our view, ethics is the driver of principled social work practice. Social work practice that is consciously informed by an ethical base offers a means to re-empower social workers to become 'ethical activists'—professional practitioners working for social justice and human wellbeing.

This idea of ethics as empowerment grew out of our realisation while teaching and talking to both novitiate and experienced practitioners in Australia, Canada, the United States and the United Kingdom that social workers were experiencing a loss of their professional ethical identity. In short, social workers felt ethically disempowered. Given that many definitions of disempowerment or powerlessness refer to the control or lack of control persons have over their environment and their destiny (Mullaly 1997; McArdle 1998), we could see the irony in a profession that has empowerment of clients and citizens as one of its central tenets but then seems powerless to act in its own professional ethical interests.

The idea that social workers are, themselves, disempowered is of course not a new one (Mullaly 1997). Nevertheless our conversations with practitioners told us that something had changed over the past two decades. Over this period, globalisation, neo-liberalism and so-called new managerialism have brought greater bureaucratic accountability, coupled with greater specialisation and fragmentation of professional roles, all of which have impacted in some way on professional life (Banks 1998). At the level of practice, the imposition of risk management polices and decision-making protocols have both contributed to the feeling, real or apparent, that professional judgement, discretion and autonomy have been diminished or lost. Moreover, the fear of legal accountability or legal risk, and the adoption of risk aversion or defensive practice have further helped to undermine professional autonomy (Collingridge 1991).

In a conversation with a group of Australian social workers, when asked how all these changes had impinged on the way they worked, the universal response was that they now tended 'to follow the rule book'— those departmental policies and protocols established to deal with cases. As one worker observed, 'If you follow the rules, even if they are not in the best interests of your clients, they can't get you, and if they try, you can shift all responsibility back on to the department.' Attitudes such as this lend support to Rhodes' claim that human service organisations undermine 'ordinary concepts of morality', suggesting the impossibility of ethical practice (Rhodes 1986). In an environment that is in many ways hostile to professional ethical practice, it is little wonder questions are asked about the relevance of professional ethics to the practice of social work.

This book is in part an antidote to the pervasive thinking in some social work writing that nothing can be done either to alleviate the material conditions of practice or to fill the philosophical vacuum created once ethics is deemed irrelevant to professional life. The main argument of this book is that a coherent ethical framework based on our concept of ethical practice offers the social work profession and workers within the welfare sector a way forward. We argue that an ethically articulate profession must have a base from which to reassert its moral imperative to advocate for social justice and human wellbeing. In the current climate, developing an active commitment to a common set of ethical principles and values is the key factor in forging a new identity for social work as a force for change.

As part of addressing the question 'What makes a good social worker?' we assert that social workers must become ethical activists, in a similar way that Yeatman defines a 'policy activist' as:

anyone who champions in relatively consistent ways a value orientation and pragmatic commitment to . . . the policy process . . . which opens it up to the appropriate participation of all those involved in policy all the way through points of conception, operational formulation, implementation, delivery on the ground, consumption and evaluation (Yeatman 1998: 34).

Social work practice that incorporates ethics as its core, and invites participation from all involved in the process, inevitably involves working against dominant policy agendas that are inimical to good ethical outcomes. Ethical social work practice, then, is not just about a disposition to act ethically in professional contexts, but also a desire to actively challenge and change those contexts or policy environments by an ethically articulate profession. To deny this is to diminish the professional project implicit in all human service work.

The relationship between ethics, values and codes

In this book we use codes of ethics as the basis for discussing social work values, principles and ethical practice. We choose this path because, on their own, values are relatively weak. There is no agreed set of social work values apart from published codes of ethics. Codes of ethics on the other hand systematise values, and provide a framework from which to develop a shared understanding of social work ethics. Another reason why codes of ethics are central to this book is our belief that codes can be used as a tool for empowering social work to achieve its purpose. In order for this to happen, however, social work has to bring ethics in from the margins of its identity and understand that ethics is the heart of social work itself.

Terminology and focus of the book

Several of the terms used in this book require introduction. First, throughout the book we (the four authors) refer to ourselves as 'we'. This book represents our collective voice—we have all worked on the chapters and reached consensus on the points therein. While in different chapters the tone might alter as one or another of us expresses these thoughts on behalf of the rest, we still feel justified in using the plural pronoun to refer to our 'voice'.

Another potentially problematic term is the one used for people with whom social workers work. Following in the footsteps of social work writers such as Malcolm Payne (2005) and Jim Ife (2001) we use the traditional term 'client'. For us this is a more inclusive term and one that implies a relationship with rights and responsibilities on both sides. It is also a term that implies the power differential that we believe must be acknowledged and worked with as part of ethical practice. To us, terms such as 'consumer' or 'customer' have neo-liberal undertones and imply market-type relationships that reduce people to the level of being a commodity. On the other hand, more neutral terms such as 'service user' or 'user', while prevalent in some countries, to us are too technocratic and imply either no relationship or a passive one-way relationship with an impersonal service. In some chapters we also use the terms from the literature that we are discussing, for example 'caseworker'. We recognise that different countries prefer different terms, and ask readers to use the terms that suit their contexts best when considering the arguments we raise in the book.

We also would like to acknowledge the impact of the user rights movement and its influence on professional practice which has led to the development of a partnerships approach, both to shaping the delivery of services and also codes of ethics.

While we recognise that the social work profession is mostly female, we have not adopted a firm rule on whether we refer to individuals as she or he, other than when obviously referring to a female or male.

This book is about ethical social work practice generally and provides a framework from which to consider specific practice situations. It won't tell you how to practice within particular practice settings, for example with the elderly or child welfare, but does give a concrete framework of virtues, skills and knowledge that can be applied to all dimensions of social work practice from therapeutic work with individuals and families through to community development, research and policy work. Similarly the book is not aimed at analysing specific issues that impact on social work practice such as race and gender. The universal and pluralist approach employed incorporates principles that can be applied to the more detailed analysis of specific issues and practice settings.

Structure of the book

Ethical Practice in Social Work is divided into four sections. We begin by examining the challenges social work faces in its present context. In line with Payne's (2005) thinking about the main arenas influencing social work, we discuss the political-social-ideological context in chapter 1 and the agency-professional context in chapter 2. We conclude Part One by considering the challenges ethics poses to social work, and what it means when we discuss 'ethical social work practice'. Chapter 3 also introduces specific ethical theories, and the pluralistic approach which treats these theories as modes of complex ethical reasoning. Part Two examines social work's response to these challenges, in particular its ethical base expressed in codes of ethics and the principles of human rights and human dignity, and social justice. Part Three looks more closely at ethical practice in the third arena of social work identified by Payne (2005): the client-worker-agency arena. Finally, the book concludes with a summary of the elements needed for ethical social work practice. This includes the virtues, knowledge and skills that we develop throughout the book that together enable social workers and the social work profession to be empowered to act in the world and to make ethical decisions.

Each chapter begins with case studies from which underlying principles are developed. The case studies are either based on real-life examples or composites of our own and others' experiences. They have been gathered over the course of our own and our colleagues' teaching in, and practising, social work. Our intention is to motivate discussion on the issues by showing how theoretical discussions arise from real-world problems, and also how the problems we encounter can be resolved in practice.

In addition to the central content of each chapter, we discuss three ethical themes: virtues, skills and knowledge. Together, these provide a framework for empowering social work practice. They demonstrate how ethics is interwoven with everyday social work concepts. The themes emerge from the content of each chapter; while not the core of each chapter they offer commentary and ways to apply the main ideas. The three themes are:

- *Virtues*—the personal qualities and character traits that go into making a good social worker. Virtue is about 'being'; when we introduce a virtue, we are inviting you to 'cultivate this way of being'. Examples of virtues include being reflective and having moral courage.
- *Ethical skills*—the techniques that connect ethics to successful social work practice. Ethical skills are about 'doing' and 'thinking'; when we discuss ethical skills, we are asking you to focus on how to do something. Examples of ethical skills include ethical decision-making and critical reasoning.
- *Ethical knowledge*—the key concepts, principles and theories needed for ethical social work practice. Ethical knowledge is about 'knowing' and 'understanding'; when we explore ethical knowledge we are asking you to learn or understand something, and to develop a core ethical vocabulary. Examples include ideas from philosophy such as teleology or thought experiments, and ideas from social work such as human rights and social justice.

The themes are gradually developed throughout the book so that by the last chapter, social workers and students will have a toolkit of virtues, knowledge and skills needed to engage in ethical practice throughout their professional lives. As you acquire ethical knowledge and skills, you will be able to develop virtues. The three themes necessarily overlap because, in most instances, virtues require corresponding ethical skills and knowledge. For example, the virtue of practical reasoning is a character trait that requires other virtues such as open-mindedness, ethical skills such as critical analysis and being able to make sound and valid arguments, and knowledge of various approaches to ethical reasoning. The themes are not meant to be taken as solid things in themselves— they are more like organising concepts for your ethical toolkit that can have fluid boundaries. There is little point worrying whether something is a skill, a virtue or a piece of knowledge; the question is rather whether it is useful to think of something in one way or another. At times, it is most useful to think of, say, critical reflection as a skill to be learnt. At other times critical reflection is usefully viewed as a character trait; we might describe someone as a reflective practitioner, and this is an attribute to which social workers aspire.

Each chapter concludes with study questions, further reading and references to websites and other resources for those who want to extend their knowledge.

We hope this is the beginning of a reinvigorated ethical conversation, within and outside social work, a conversation that places ethics at the heart of the social work profession, as its driving and defining life force. We also hope this book helps you on your journey to becoming ethically active social work practitioners.

Part one
Challenges for ethical practice

1
Social work in its environment

Gina and Harry are two friends who have recently achieved a lifelong ambition to become social workers. Gina had previously worked part-time as a voluntary counsellor with a telephone crisis service, while bringing up her two children. Harry had transferred from studying a degree in science into the social work degree. They became firm friends after meeting in a tutorial in first year, discovering they lived near each other, and sharing transport to the university over the next few years. At graduation they decided to keep in touch.

Several months after graduation they arranged to meet for their first coffee and a catch-up. They had planned to meet earlier, but could not organise a time to suit them both. Gina now works close to home at her local council as a community development officer. Harry is employed as a caseworker for the state welfare agency. Harry is an hour late for the meeting. He rushes in just as Gina is about to pay for her coffee and leave.

Apologising profusely he explains that he had gone out to investigate a report of suspected child abuse. Neighbours had telephoned the office about incessant crying they heard from the house next door. When Harry arrived, he could hear the crying but no one answered his knocking. The neighbour appeared and told him she thought that the couple who lived next door had driven away early that morning. She had heard the car go, but not seen them leave. They had three children aged four, two and nine months. The crying had started about midday and she was worried the baby had been left in the house without supervision. Harry called the police. They broke into the house and found all three children but no adults. In the lounge room the television was hissing white static, plates of half-empty food lay on the floor and mess was trampled through the house. They found the four-year-old and two-year-old hiding under a bed. The baby was in a cot together with several bottles of milk. The baby's room smelt of sour milk or vomit and dirty nappies.

The police took all three children to a local hospital for a medical check, while Harry tried to arrange emergency respite care until the parents were located and the situation sorted out. Thankfully, he found a foster family willing to have the children for the weekend.

'In my six months with the department, this is the worst I have seen,' Harry said. 'Nothing we learnt at uni prepares you for what people can do to their own kids. I tell you, Gina, finishing my science degree would have been easier than this. I wouldn't want to be in those foster parents' shoes this weekend. The four-year-old bit the police officer on the arm when she was trying to get him out from under the bed. The baby screamed when I reached out to pick her up. The smell was still in the car after we dropped them off, and they had been bathed at the hospital. Lucky those foster parents are so experienced. I wouldn't know what to do with kids like that. I hope they don't ring me for advice.

'The worst thing is, it seems like it's only downhill from here. What chances have those kids got once they're in the system? They're likely to get more difficult, get moved around, maybe split up. You know the statistics on abuse once kids go into care. How much more will these kids have to go through? It's pretty much out of my hands now. What if I have only made things worse in the long run? But I couldn't have left them where they were either.'

Gina nodded. 'The politics of community committees and submission writing seem like a picnic compared to what you are telling me. At uni I thought we were being trained to make a difference. When you're out there in the real world, though, it's more like just a fight to survive. So much work, so many expectations, so much paperwork to justify your own position. If I could just stop writing about what I want to do and get on with doing it, things would be a lot easier.'

'Yeah,' Harry responded. 'If you think red tape is bad in a council, you should try child protection. Even the questions you ask are pretty much pre-written for you, unless of course there is no one around to ask, like what happened today. In my job it's mostly a policy for this, a protocol for that, and so on. Quite a few of my colleagues don't even have a degree. Sometimes I wonder what all that education was for.'

To think about ethical practice in social work, we first have to consider what social work is, and the impact of the environment. In this chapter we argue that it is fundamentally important to understand the environment in which social work operates. Further, we argue that if we are to understand our environment, and to practise ethically, we need to have an open mind, be able to critically analyse a situation, recognise a sound argument and understand the importance of a teleological approach to ethics.

The situation in which Harry and Gina find themselves is quite common, especially for new graduates in the field. Overburdened with the amount and type of work being employed in organisations in which they are still learning how systems work, new social workers can feel overwhelmed and as though the social work they are experiencing in the real world is nothing like they expected to find while they were studying at university.

From their conversation, Gina and Harry do not seem to be at all clear about who they are as social workers or what their primary purpose is. They appear to be instinctively reacting to the demands placed on them by their environment, rather than offering a measured response informed by a clear set of values or being proactive in other ways. The very different types of work they do—submission writing and community development on one hand, and working with individuals and families involved in the child protection system on the other, illustrates just a little of the huge variety social work encompasses. To begin our book on ethical practice in social work we need an idea of what social work is, before we examine the environment in which social workers work, and some of the challenges they face.

What is social work?

One of the difficult questions social work students face is 'What do you do?' Whereas most people seem to know what teachers, nurses, doctors or lawyers do without having to ask, there does not seem to be this general understanding about social work. Social workers themselves find it a hard question to answer. Why is this so? Partly, it is difficult to encapsulate the variety and complexity of social work in a few phrases. There is not one readily identifiable function that all social workers perform such as teaching or curing the sick. Partly it is because social work itself can be invisible—social workers work in partnership with people, systems and organisations to tackle problems at various levels. It is rarely the social worker alone who does something that can be identified as being 'social work', except perhaps in notorious situations such as the removal of children. Lastly, social workers do things that many other professions also share. Counselling, working in groups, solving organisational problems, working with communities, all these are activities that other professions perform, although we argue, in different ways.

Let us see how the profession itself defines social work. In July 2000, the International Federation of Social Workers (IFSW) adopted a new definition of social work at its general meeting in Montreal, Canada:

The social work profession promotes social change, problem solving in human relationships and the empowerment and liberation of people to enhance well-being. Utilising theories of human behaviour and social systems, social work intervenes at the points where people interact with their environments. Principles of human rights and social justice are fundamental to social work (IFSW 2002).

Liberating people, empowering them, solving problems, enhancing wellbeing, promoting social change—exciting stuff. You would expect social work courses to be crammed to bursting with people keen to learn how to do these things. A profession fuelled by principles of human rights and social justice that strives for social change and liberation sounds powerful and proactive; it is the source of this power, and ways to enhance it, that we will be exploring in this book. Yet so often social workers experience the reverse: feeling disempowered, lost and at the mercy of forces much greater than themselves, as we see in the case study of Gina and Harry. Even Gina's forlorn memory that she had been trained to 'make a difference' is a pale reflection of the 2000 IFSW definition.

Ideas such as liberation, social change or empowerment are complex and abstract. Even the more moderate and often cited response, also appearing in the definition above, that social workers intervene 'between people and their environments' does not adequately capture the complex enterprise that is social work, nor the vision that drives it. However, being abstract and complex is not sufficient to explain why it is so difficult for social workers to explain what they do. The environment has an enormous impact, as implied in the quote from the definition, because social workers work between people and their environments. Indeed Healy asserts:

The deeply contextual nature of social work differentiates it from other professions. Our professional practice foundations— our knowledge, purpose and skills bases—are substantially constructed in, and through, the environments in which we work (Healy 2005: 4).

In order to understand the nature of social work, including the apparent contradictions between its visionary aims, the work-day realities which many social workers experience and their consequent inability to articulate what they do, we not only need to understand the environments in which we work, we need to be able to work *with* these environments. Fook (2002: 161–2) argues that by accepting the importance and strong influence of environments ('reframing our practice as contextual'), social workers no longer need to treat their environments as givens. Instead they can learn to work with their environments, taking responsibility for some parts and seeing possibilities for change within them, even in small areas. She argues:

> Our practice is simply defined as *working with the context*, no matter what that context may be. If we perceive our environments as hostile, then we simply work to change this, rather than trying to work in spite of it. The focus becomes one of changing the environment, or aspects of it, rather than seeing ourselves as a 'crusader' or 'victim' role, as the lone person prevented from doing their job because of their environment (Fook 2002: 161–2).

Neither Gina nor Harry seems to have this idea of working with their environments. Instead they see themselves as victims, each alone in their hostile circumstances. Working alone can be lonely and exacerbate the sense of futility—why bother trying to change something that cannot be changed? However, if we appreciate that other social workers are in the same position and if each of us tries to address the context of practice, our collective efforts can produce change.

The first task of our book, then, is to examine social work in its environments. Payne argues that three arenas are particularly important in influencing what social work is. One is the *political-social-ideological arena*, in which social and political debate forms the policy that guides agencies and the purposes they are set or develop for themselves' (Payne 2005: 17). The second is the *agency-professional arena*, in which employers and employees influence each other about the more specific aspects of how social work operates. The third is the *client-worker-agency arena* in which clients, workers and agencies all influence each other to produce the activity known as social work. Payne emphasises that each of these arenas influences the other two and gives examples of how clients and social workers can influence all three arenas.

In Part One of this book we examine the political-social-ideological arena (chapter 1) and the agency-professional arena (chapter 2), looking at the challenges social work faces and the notions of power that go with them, before we explore in Part Two (chapters 4 and 5) the heart of social work and the source of power it can draw on to become the profession pictured in the IFSW definition. Part Three examines in more detail the client-worker-agency arena as we consider ethical practice in social work.

The political-social-ideological arena: Postmodernism

Gina and Harry are not alone in their doubts about social work, and in their questioning of what impact individual social workers can have. Many authors have identified how the social work profession is facing new challenges and opportunities in the globalised, postmodern world in which we find ourselves (Adams, Dominelli and Payne 2002; Fook 2002; Hugman 2003; Ife 1997; Alston and McKinnon 2001, 2005). The term 'postmodern' is used in two ways that are closely related. On one hand it refers to a family of theoretical approaches, or methods, for understanding and analysing the political-social-ideological arena in which we live. On the other hand, 'postmodern' is a term that identifies our current times, as against previous eras.

Drawing on the work of Bauman (1995), Hugman (2005: 2–10) describes four main periods in the history of social and religious thought, all of which influence our postmodern era in some way. The first was the classical era, during Greek and Roman times, during which the foundations of western philosophical thought were laid down. The second was the medieval period, in which the ideas from the classical era were interwoven with Christian and Judaic religious threads (monotheism). The third period was modernity, or the 'age of reason'. It was then that scientific thought began to replace a religious understanding of the social world—'the era of classic liberal philosophy in which ethics started to become the science of moral life, in the context of the rapid development of industrial society' (Hugman 2005: 3). We will explore some of the ethical theories from the modern era in more detail in chapter 3. Social work is a product of modernity; it is one of the secular replacements for the welfare role of the Christian church in western countries and, reflecting its liberal underpinnings, it is based on the modern idea that we can reach a rational understanding of people and societies, and take rational action to deal with the problems we see (Payne 2005: 15).

The fourth era is 'postmodernity'. In contrast to modernity's certainty about the world, and its use of scientific proof to test competing theories, postmodernity is a time of uncertainty, fragmentation, plurality and diversity (Hugman 2005). In social work one example is the fragmentation and increasing specialisation of social work that we discuss later in this chapter. There are many families of postmodern approaches, just as there are competing modernist approaches. Whereas all modernist approaches require a notion of objective 'truth' as the standard by which we can judge whether one state of affairs or idea is better than others (Hugman 2003; Ife 1997), all postmodern approaches share a belief that there is no such thing as objective 'truth'. Instead of using scientific method to know about our world, postmodernism views knowledge itself as constructed by human beings through language, and so is more interested in understanding language and how it creates meaning and relationships of power and dominance. Hugman (2005) points out that the scepticism and uncertainty of the postmodern era are leading to a rediscovery of earlier periods, plus attempts to synthesise competing ideas from other eras. He highlights the 'rediscovery' of the ancient Greek tradition, particularly the work of Aristotle with a new emphasis on virtue ethics, in professional ethics writings of the 1990s. Indeed, virtue-based ethics form an important foundation for the approach to ethical practice in social work in this book.

Discourse

One of the most useful tools to emerge from postmodern analysis is the notion of discourse. Fook defines discourse as 'the ways in which we make meanings of and construct our world through the language we use (verbal and non-verbal) to communicate about it' (Fook 2002: 63). Drawing on the work of Foucault, Fook explains that the notion of discourse includes not only beliefs and ideas, but also social practices, our ideas of who we are and power relations.

Dominant discourses are like tinted lenses that colour our world, without us knowing that we are wearing glasses. They incorporate the ideas and power relations that we take for granted. For example, the mother of one of the authors (Wendy's mother), who is a teacher committed to addressing social injustice, particularly racism, looks back in amazement at her childhood. She grew up in a country town in a loving Christian environment that taught her to care for others, yet at the same time, no one questioned that the indigenous people in her community lived on the edge of the rubbish dump, excluded from even the basic benefits that the white citizens of the town enjoyed. It was just 'the way things are', part of the 'natural' order. This example illustrates not only the power of a dominant discourse, but also the usefulness of the idea. Once we begin to understand how we internalise discourses and how they shape our realities, we can also begin to question things we have previously taken for granted and to analyse our environment from different perspectives. In our globalised world we have many oppor-tunities to recognise the dominant discourses affecting us, and how they operate. For example, travelling or meeting someone from another culture might help us see that we have taken certain things for granted

(Gardner 2006). Closer to home are debates such as those around what is a family, and whether homosexual couples with children should be included in that definition (Payne 2005).

However, most of the time we exist within discourses without recognising their pervasive influence. If we stop to think, we could all identify an experience such as the one Wendy's mother describes. One of the discourses that is particularly dominant at this time in the English-speaking West, and gaining momentum in other parts of the world, is the neo-liberal discourse. Neo-liberalism, which shares many of the values of classical liberalism (Waligorski 1997), first made its presence felt in the mid-1970s following the 1973 oil crisis. Central to neo-liberalism is the person as an autonomous being who has the right to do as they see fit, provided no other person is harmed by their actions. In this context, liberty is the absence of any form of restraint, including legal sanctions, which may prevent a person from acting as they wish. Thus liberty is based on each person having control over what they do and knowing best how to advance their own happiness.

Waligorski (1997) suggests that neo-liberals believe that:

- through competitive neutrality and a value-free context the market is able to solve all social problems such as discrimination and the need for regulation of financial institutions, unsafe working conditions and poor education (and so there is no need for equal opportunity or anti-discrimination legislation for example);
- only competition can control self-interest through equality of exchanges in the market, while any inequality that arises out of the operation of the market can be justified on the grounds of 'natural' differences (and so there is no need for government to intervene to protect people who are poor, have disabilities etc.);
- welfare and social services create dependence and weakness, promote crime, riots, promiscuity and in doing so destroy freedom and independence (for example, the belief that young women deliberately fall pregnant in order to receive social security benefits);
- public policy should not be used to influence the economy (for

example there is no need for the government to intervene in setting minimum wage levels, or having arbitration systems for disputes about wages); and
- all government 'think tanks' and committees on managing the economy should be dissolved (and have been in many western countries in recent years).

Given the above it is not surprising that neo-liberals seek to curb the power and sphere of influence of government. Instead, they believe that the market, through competition, should be allowed to take all decisions surrounding the regulation of social relationships and the formulation of social policy.

Power

Sprinkled throughout our discussions on discourse, on neo-liberalism and in just about everything written about social work, is the word 'power'. Heywood (2000: 35) defines power broadly 'as the ability to achieve a desired outcome, sometimes referred to . . . as the "power *to*" do something'. You will find more specific definitions in different contexts. Thus, as Heywood notes (p. 35), in the political arena 'power . . . is usually thought of as [being associated with] a relationship . . . and of having power over others'.

Associated with power is the notion of empowerment. This is identified in the IFSW's definition of social work as one of the means of enhancing individual and collective wellbeing. Whether we like it or not, social workers have to deal with power in daily practice. The problem, as Pakulski neatly puts it, is that 'power is a slippery concept: it is both general and fluid, and therefore contestable' (Pakulski 2004: 22). Pakulski notes that liberal analysts tend to see power as limited to 'politics' whereas more radical critics see power as permeating all aspects of social relations. For example, more radical writers look at how institutions are structured, who benefits from 'the rules of the game', and how power relations are inherent in various discourses and everyday interactions. One thing about which both liberal and radical views agree, however, is that power can be exercised directly through domination or force, as well as indirectly through influence (Pakulski 2004: 22).

How we understand power and empowerment depends on our political and theoretical perspectives. Payne highlights the contrasting ways three different views of social work see empowerment. Coming from social democratic philosophy is the reflexive-therapeutic view. This focuses on notions of personal empowerment, and how through mutual interaction social workers and clients influence each others' ideas and respond to social concerns, increase their personal power and overcome disadvantage (a view that resonates with a focus on individual wellbeing and some forms of human rights). On the other hand, coming from socialist political philosophy is the socialist-collective view, also known as an emancipatory or transformational approach. This perspective sees power as being held by elites or particular groups within institutions in society that oppress other groups. Thus empowerment is about transforming society and its institutions for the benefit of the poorest and most oppressed (a view that has a corresponding emphasis on social justice and the more collective definitions of human rights). Quite a different approach comes from liberal and neo-liberal political philosophy. This approach in social work, termed by Payne the individualist-reformist view, sees social work as maintaining the existing social order and helping individuals through particular periods of difficulty they may be experiencing (adapted from Payne 2005: 8–9). This view does not consider empowerment directly; it expects market forces to sort out who has power and who does not.

Payne points out that while these different views compete with each other, they also have affinities and in fact nearly all social work positions contain different mixtures of each. For example in our case study, it is most likely that the welfare department Harry works for operates somewhere between an individualist-reformist and reflexive-therapeutic perspective, with very little emphasis on seeking to change structures or questioning the power of the Department to intervene.

Gina, on the other hand, might see power somewhere between the individualist-reformist and socialist-collective positions. While she may seek major change in the lives of the people in her community by getting them to work collectively, in fact the committees she works with are most likely to establish services such as self-help playgroups within existing social arrangements, rather than trying to change them.

Fook argues for a view of power that encompasses micro (personal) and macro (social) levels, and that sees power as both good and bad (Fook 2002: 52-3). She points out that social structures simultaneously empower and disempower people; for example, Harry in our case study feels disempowered as a worker, and yet is empowered to intervene and take children from a house. Fook also argues that people can use and create power wherever they are, and that the key for social workers is to understand how power is expressed, experienced and created by different people at different levels (Fook 2002: 53).

Social workers need to understand that power works in two main ways, according to Chenoweth and McAuliffe. First, social workers must understand that many of the people they work with are disempowered by experiences and systems. Second, they need to understand the dynamics of power in their working relationships. These authors emphasise that there is an unavoidable power imbalance between practitioners and clients; that social workers need to be aware of how they exercise the power and authority they hold; and that it is important to understand that power takes many forms (Chenoweth and McAuliffe 2005: 35–41). Along with Fook (2002) they warn of the dangers of a simplistic approach to empowerment, and that it can in fact lead to further disempowering the very people social workers are trying to empower.

Social work in the postmodern environment

Having considered some of the broader aspects of the political-social-ideological arena, in particular the neo-liberal discourse as well as how we view postmodernism and its treatment of concepts such as power, we now examine in more detail some of the challenges that our postmodern environment poses for social work. Globalisation, which is described by Tabb (2001: 13) as the process by which 'events and activities in one part of the world come to have significant consequences' for others, is integral to neo-liberalism, and impacts on social workers at many levels. Just ask your teachers how social work jobs have changed in the last thirty or so years. When Wendy began practising as a social worker in the late 1970s, she entered a world of established social work departments, where people had held the same job for ten years and more. These days many social work departments have shrunk or 'downsized'. Some organisations which used to have social work departments have restructured into multi-disciplinary teams, based around stages of life or particular issues. Social workers along with many other occupational groups are members of these teams. In such organisations, while the social work departments may have disappeared, there is a wide variety of jobs for which social workers may compete along with other occupational groups. In other large organisations, social work has been centralised into a major career choice, with job progression and professional development available in a variety of social work positions within the one organisation. Generally though, instead of expecting to spend years in one job, social workers can expect to hold several positions during their working life. The advent of short-term contracts to service providers means short-term employment for many people, available only for the life of the contract.

In her excellent overview of the postmodern context of social work, Fook (2002: 19–30) examines some of the economic, technological, theoretical and political changes that globalisation has brought. She emphasises that there are many contradictions in the effects of globalisation. For example, on one hand globalisation can be seen as being responsible for unifying and compressing social differences, on the other for causing social fragmentation and exacerbating inequality, a view shared by Pakulski (2004).

Economically, Fook (2002) argues that international globalisation results in shrinking public welfare and a growth in privatisation, which lead to increased competition between service providers. 'Purchaser-provider split' means that providers competing for contracts and involved with the service users become separated from the policy-makers on the purchaser side of the divide. This results in short-term contracts, 'marketised' services, and a focus on specific outcomes and programs so that professional knowledge becomes conceptualised in relation to specific services rather than generic professional orientation. Within this environment there is less welfare money and resources going to ever more closely targeted groups. Bisman (2004) documents the widening gap between advantaged and disadvantaged people, both within and between countries. Gaps in income rates, health and education levels, and employment are all widening with ever-increasing percentages of people in the disadvantaged category. The policies that lead to these economic changes are all designed to minimise the role of the state in providing services (and the cost of doing so) and thus are part of the neo-liberal agenda. The fact that they are now so widespread, across so many countries, demonstrates the dominance of this discourse.

Technological changes also offer challenges and possibilities. On one hand new computer technology and the internet have the potential to reduce isolation and bring resources to previously disadvantaged groups, create new communities and improve service provision and standards. On the other there are new possibilities for disadvantaged groups to be created, and for more monitoring of professionals' work, while computer systems have the potential to take over professional skills and undermine autonomy (for example, computer-driven counselling models).

New ways of thinking have also come about as globalisation and new technologies break down the traditional hierarchies, the nature of professions and the organisation of modernist knowledge. Fook (2002) claims that this enables a plurality and diversity of perspectives to be valued—for example qualitative perspectives in research, and the views of service users and 'the ordinary person' or group are now recognised as important points of view to be taken into account. Similarly Healy (2004) and Khinduka (2004) argue that globalisation brings opportunities as well as threats—that the voices of previously silenced groups can now be heard, and that diversity and plurality can be valued as never before.

Banks (1998) identifies four main elements of the postmodern world which she claims seriously challenge the traditional view of social work as a profession with an agreed set of values. These include the increasing fragmentation and specialisation of social workers, so that they have less and less in common with each other; the growth of proceduralisation, with the massive increase in detailed guidelines, checklists, agency-based codes of practice and procedures (the things that Harry in our case study complains about) that undermine the ability of social workers to make autonomous decisions and exercise professional discretion based on their assessment of a situation; the changing roles of social workers, from traditional casework, group work and community development to resource management, assessment and monitoring; and finally, the rise of service users' power in social work service delivery, which demands that service users be involved in decision-making about their services, and that the nature of social work services be changed to a more impersonal 'contract' based on consumer rights rather than the traditional relationship of professional expertise and trust.

In later writing, Banks (2002) brings these themes together when she argues that the increasing pressure on social workers to be accountable for their decisions and actions is squeezing social work practice in particular ways. Banks (2002: 28–9) distinguishes two types of accountability: professional accountability to service users, which is integral to the core values of social work; and public accountability to organisations and the public at large. In an environment that demands ever greater public accountability, professional accountability to service users is being sacrificed (Banks 2002: 36–7). Thus social workers are having to spend more and more time on bureaucratic and detailed procedures such as filling in endless forms (public accountability) instead of having time for the more traditional means of being accountable to service users, such as routine recording of decisions in files, and reflective discussions during supervision about their actions with service users. The emphasis on public accountability can lead to defensive practice, with individuals worried about 'watching their backs' to avoid being blamed and avoiding taking risks. Banks (2002: 37) concludes that we need to re-focus our attention on communicating with service users, honestly recognise potential conflicts and power differentials, and strive to change the culture of organisations so that they take responsibility when things go wrong, rather than seeking to blame a particular individual.

Bauman (2000) points out that, through the kinds of processes outlined above (increasing specialisation, bureaucracy and regulation), postmodern society provides all kinds of structures to help us avoid our responsibilities to each other. Increasingly complex bureaucracies and work specialisations assist us to avoid seeing the big picture. Instead we follow the expectation that we simply concentrate on the tiny part for which we are responsible. As long as someone keeps the train running on time, it is not their responsibility what the cargo might be even if it is human beings headed for extermination camps. Bauman (2000) also argues that increasingly complex and specific codes of ethics, laws and regulations invite us to avoid responsibility. As long as we follow the letter of the law or policy, we think we are doing the right thing and don't have to worry about the larger picture.

The increasing complexity and specialisation of the postmodern world also means that we are ever more interdependent with each other. Bauman (2000) points out that in this context, when neo-liberals rail against 'welfare dependency' they are actually attacking morality itself (the responsibility to care for each other). We need to recognise our increasing interdependence on each other, and the highly political and misleading nature of terms such as 'welfare dependency'.

Despite the challenges posed by the globalised, postmodern environment to all the professions, we feel that social workers are particularly well placed to meet these new demands within the present uncertainty, fragmentation and changing local contexts. After all, as we have seen in the IFSW definition, social work is one of the few professions which aims to intervene 'at the points where people interact with their environment' (IFSW 2002), and thus it is part of our main focus to understand and deal with changing local contexts and uncertainty. Like Banks (2002), Fook (2002) and Healy (2004) also emphasise the importance of interpersonal and communication skills in the postmodern world—another strength of social work.

What is ethics?

Ethics is a practical matter, just as it was for the ancient Greeks. It is about deciding what to do and acting on that decision. We explain the nature of ethics in more detail in chapter 3. By way of introduction however, we note that in our view, social work ethics is NOT about how to be good, but rather about how to 'work well' towards the goals of social work. This idea means that in order to judge whether we are acting ethically as social workers, we need to be clear about social work's goals. As well as taking our goals into account, we also believe that how we achieve them, or the means we use are equally important. Further, social workers should be encouraged to develop certain character traits and discouraged from developing others. Thus we will be arguing for a pluralistic approach to ethical practice, one that incorporates aspects of virtue, utilitarian and deontological approaches. All of these we examine in more detail in chapter 3.

Ethics in postmodern social work

Almost paradoxically, the postmodern world has created a new place for ethics in social work. Bauman (2000) argues that this is because up until the postmodern era, there were both economic and moral reasons for having welfare and for caring for disadvantaged groups. Economically it made sense to maintain a large, healthy pool of poor people as a 'reserve army' of labour or potential soldiers who could step in when necessary to keep up production or to protect the nation-state. There was also the moral argument: that we are a social species who care for each other and that the heart of morality is that we are 'our brother's keeper'. However, in postmodern times, with new technologies creating change in industrial and agricultural production as well as sophisticated military weaponry, there is no longer the need for such a large reserve of healthy disadvantaged people nor for mass armies. Only the moral argument remains—that we should be our 'brother's keeper' and take responsibility for each other, whether the other deserves it or not, and regardless of whether they have something to offer us in return.

Without the economic arguments to justify caring for each other, social work is left as a solely moral endeavour, in an environment that actively undermines that morality. Bauman (2000) asserts that the social and work structures of postmodern societies powerfully invite us to avoid our responsibilities to each other, while overt arguments mounted by neo-liberals against 'welfare dependency' disguise the actual interdependency we all share. This leaves social work in a difficult position. Ife (1997) points out that in such an environment, simply being a social worker is now a radical activity. Bauman (2000) concludes that 'being a social worker means having great moral courage'.

Bauman's analysis about how social work has become a moral activity in the postmodern world gives new meaning to similar, older claims by social work writers, such as Younghusband (1970), Butrym (1976), Clark and Asquith (1985) and Watson and Leighton (1985). More recently, many authors now advocate a new involvement in social work ethics. They advocate 'translating', 'communicating', 'questioning', 're-positioning' and 're-focusing' what social work values are, and discussing these values with service users and employing organisations (Banks 1998, 2002; Dominelli 2002; Fook 2002; Hugman 2003).

Thus we argue that ethics is the heart of social work practice. Ethics is also its source of power. With ethics as its centre, social work can become the profession envisioned in the IFSW definition: enhancing human wellbeing, promoting social change, working to solve problems and realising human rights and social justice. How can we make ethics the centre of social work practice in the real world? This book proposes a strategy with several strands. One of these is that a framework that builds ethical virtues, ethical skills and ethical knowledge will give us the tools required. In each chapter we introduce various virtues, skills and knowledge that together construct a matrix that conceptualise ethics as the power source of social work.

Virtues

We have discussed how virtue theories, which were the mainstay of ethics in the ancient world, have enjoyed a renaissance in recent times. In chapter 3 we will discuss in more detail virtue ethics as one of the main approaches to ethics in social work practice. For the purposes of this chapter, however, it is important to understand that the idea of virtue, as originally conceived by Aristotle, is about character traits or personal qualities, i.e. the kind of person you are. When we discuss virtues throughout this book, we are inviting you to 'cultivate this way of being'.

Hugman (2005: 4) points out that the Greek philosophers believed that virtues are not just natural qualities that you either have or do not have; virtues can be taught and developed through practice. By focusing on virtues in this book, we also assume that virtues or character traits can be learned and developed.

The first virtue, which we have introduced in this chapter by implication, is open-mindedness. If we are to change from having our perception of reality being completely shaped by the dominant discourse, if we are to be open to seeing how to work with our environment instead of despite it, we need to cultivate an open mind. This is not easy, as we saw in the case of Harry and Gina that began this chapter. Despite their best intentions they both became victims of their work environment, reacting to its pressures, complaining about its shortcomings, but not seeing it as a site for change. We will always be enslaved to our prejudices, enculturated values, old habits and environments unless we can consider alternatives and try to see things from the perspective of others. Perspective involves more than just respecting divergent views; it also means imaginatively occupying the positions of others and seeing how our choices might impact on their very different interests and priorities. It also means appreciating that there are views of situations other than those shaped by the dominant discourse. Harry will need this virtue if he is going to put himself in the shoes of the parents in the case study, and really understand what was happening from their perspective, as well as from the children's.

There are several ingredients we need if we are to cultivate an open mind and come to an understanding of our environments. We need some ethical skills and knowledge, which we begin to discuss in the next sections. We also need to be committed to becoming more self-aware, to developing ourselves, so that we can remove internal barriers that prevent us from really understanding other people's perspectives. Social workers have themselves as their primary professional tool—they need to constantly refine this tool if they are to develop the virtue of having an open mind.

Ethical skills

Ethical skills are techniques or abilities that are required for ethical social work practice. When we discuss ethical skills, we are asking you to focus on learning how to do something. In this chapter one of the key skills needed to understand the context of social work is critical analysis. Throughout your social work education and later in your professional practice, you will continue to develop this skill. Critical analysis involves the skill of learning how to question the assumptions that inform social work practice, to think about more than black and white alternatives, to understand that there are always other possibilities. One of the building blocks of critical analysis is knowing the rules of informal logic and what constitutes a valid argument.

The word 'argument' conjures images of conflict. However in philosophy an argument is simply the logical presentation of the reasons that support a conclusion, showing how these reasons lead to the conclusion. The purpose of an argument is either to persuade someone that a certain view is true, or to persuade them that your own position is a reasonable one to hold. The latter purpose is called justification. Arguments intended to justify an ethical position are very important because we cannot always expect to persuade people, especially if the ethical positions you and they hold are based in moral beliefs that cannot be criticised or defended logically. Justification is the process by which we show others, especially the stakeholders who are affected by our choices, that we have acted from the right reasons, have taken all the right circumstances into account, and have considered everyone's interests.

The first step in producing good arguments is to ensure that our reasoning is valid. Validity is a formal property, a result of logical analysis. An argument is valid if the reasons (premises) that have been advanced really do lead to the supposed conclusion. A popular form of argument is called a deductive syllogism. Deduction is the process of drawing conclusions about an individual case from known facts about general classes. A simple syllogism has a major and minor premise. The major premise is a claim about a class of things, and the minor premise is a claim about the properties of some example supposedly belonging to that class. A common example is:

> Major premise: All ducks quack (class: ducks; claim: all members
> of the class quack)
> Minor premise: Donald quacks
> Conclusion: Donald is a duck

This argument is invalid. The invalidity comes from the fact that while it may be true that all ducks quack, it has not been proved that only ducks quack. So Donald may be a duck, but he could also be some other type of quacking thing (such as a logic professor trying to prove a point). Here's a real-world example of a slightly different kind of argument, known as an inductive syllogism. Induction is the process of drawing conclusions about groups from observing its members. This is generally not as strong as deduction because the results rely on probability.

Premise: Every graffiti artist we've arrested wears a hooded top
Premise: Every joy rider we've arrested wears a hooded top
Premise: Every train surfer we've arrested wears a hooded top
Conclusion: Everyone who wears a hooded top is a juvenile
delinquent

This too is invalid. Anyone who knows how many hooded tops are sold and compares these figures to the crime statistics can see why. If the conclusion had been simply that juvenile criminals like hooded tops then it would have been quite valid, but trivial.

Validity can be proven by logicians, but all you need to know is that there are ways that reasons do or do not support conclusions, and ensure that you order your reasons in the right ways to avoid mistakes like these.

Here's a valid argument. Can you see why it is valid? In chapter 2 we will see how it can be valid but still wrong.

Major premise: All social workers drink heavily at the pub on
Friday afternoons
Minor premise: Mikaela is a social worker
Conclusion: Mikaela drinks heavily at the pub on Friday after-
noons

Ethical knowledge

The third strand in our matrix of ethical social work practice is ethical knowledge. When we discuss ethical knowledge, we are asking you to learn or understand a particular concept in social work ethics. In this chapter, we have introduced indirectly the concept of teleology. Teleology, or the study of goals or purpose, goes right back to Aristotle, who argued that all things have an end or 'telos' towards which they move and against which they are measured. The telos of a hammer is to drive in nails. A good hammer is one that has everything needed to do this well. It will be sturdy, well balanced, sit easily in the hand, and so forth. Thus, we need to know what the goal of social work is before we can know when and to what extent we have succeeded in reaching it. This use of practical reason (also known as ends-means reasoning) is called the teleological approach to ethics.

While there are several distinct schools or modes of ethical thinking, the teleological approach is particularly central to professional ethics because, to the extent that professional ethics is about anything more than ordinary ethics, it is about the practicalities of doing the job well. A profession is defined by its goals and derives its ethics from the moral weight attached to them. Therefore, vocational ethics involves discussion of the relative importance of some vocation's goals and then a discussion of how those goals can best be met. These two related concerns form the focus of this book. The 'good' social worker is someone who understands the goals of her profession and is well equipped to achieve them. In our discussion of Harry and Gina's plight, we argued that they did not have a clear idea of the telos of social work, nor how to achieve it. In chapters 4 and 5 we address these questions in more detail.

Conclusion

In this chapter we have sketched the social-political-ideological environment in which social work operates. We have looked at some of the forces pushing social work in various directions in our postmodern, globalised environment, and have argued that understanding the context of social work is central if we are to understand social work itself. We have also argued that recognising that ethics is central to social work is now more important than ever. Flowing from this discussion, we have identified an ethical virtue (open-mindedness), ethical skills (critical analysis and sound argument) and ethical knowledge (teleology). When we combine open-mindedness, skills of critical analysis and sound argument and an understanding of teleology, we have the things we need for exercising good judgement. Good judgement is one of the fundamental virtues that Aristotle identified. If you want to develop good judgement, you need education and practical experience. In the following chapters we will explore further what makes good judgement. We will also gradually introduce the virtues, skills and knowledge required for you to become an ethical social work practitioner.

Study tasks

1 What do you think social work should be about: to maintain the status quo; to help people overcome problems; to remove the causes of oppression and promote social justice; or a little of all? Write a statement describing your vision of what you think social work should aim to achieve.

2 Have you experienced anyone who works 'with' the environment in the way that is discussed in this chapter? How is what they do different from someone who accepts that the environment is a 'given' and cannot be changed?

3 Have you had experiences like Wendy's mother, where you have discovered that what you thought was 'true' or 'natural' was actually a perception heavily influenced by the dominant discourse? Write about or discuss with a colleague how your assumptions or perceptions have changed with this realisation.

4 How do you feel about neo-liberal values and do they have a place in social work practice? Is it a suitable philosophy to inform social work practice or can you suggest a more suitable one?

5 From your experience of welfare and human service organisations, either during a practicum or as a worker, volunteer or client, which of the following trends (discussed in this chapter) have you noticed in the workplace:

   - increasing specialisation,
   - detailed regulations,
   - fragmentation of services between many organisations,
   - purchase-provider splits (the organisation providing the

funding and setting the policy is different from the organisation providing the service),
*   short-term contracts.

What impacts do these trends have on the clients of the service,
and on the workers providing the services? How has the delivery
of services been affected? Discuss these questions with your
colleagues and those experiencing these trends, and write down
your thoughts about the influence of globalisation and neo-
liberalism on the provision of social work and welfare services.

6   How does globalisation affect your life? Write down four or five
changes or aspects of your daily life that can be attributed to
globalisation.

7   What virtues do you need to cultivate in order to become a good
social worker? Write a list now and put it away. When you have
finished this book, we will suggest that you make another list and
compare it with the one you make now, to see how your ideas
have developed.

8   As an exercise in critical reasoning, find a recent press article
concerning the welfare system. An article dealing with government
policy will probably be best. Identify an argument contained within
it, and try to write it out in the structured way demonstrated in the
skills section above. Identify the premises and see how they are
supposed to support the conclusion. Do you think it is a deductive
or inductive argument? Without worrying too much about formal
criteria, describe how successful you think the argument is.

Further reading

Adams, R., Dominelli, L. and Payne, M. (eds) 2002, *Critical Practice in
Social Work*, Palgrave, Basingstoke, Hampshire. Beginning with an
excellent discussion on values and critical practice by a number of

well-known social work writers in ethics, this book contains many good articles about social work practice, mostly from a British perspective.

Alexandra, A., Matthews, S. and Miller, S. 2002, *Reasons, Values and Institutions*, Tertiary Press, Croydon. An excellent beginner's guide to informal logic, critical reasoning, and their application to thinking about ethics.

Allen, J., Pease, B. and Briskman, L. (eds) 2003, *Critical Social Work*, Allen & Unwin, Sydney. This book contains a range of articles in different aspects of social work practice.

Fook, J. 2002, *Social Work Critical Theory and Practice*, Sage, London; Thousand Oaks, New Delhi. Part one of this book (chapters 1 and 2) look at the current context of social work in detail. Many of Jan Fook's arguments are summarised in the chapter you have just read.

Gray, J. 1995, *Liberalism* (2nd edn), University of Minnesota Press, Minneapolis. Explores liberalism under conditions of modernity and post-modernism.

Healy, K. 2004, 'Social Workers in the New Human Services Marketplace: Trends, challenges and responses', *Australian Social Work*, vol. 57, no. 2, pp. 103–14. This article succinctly addresses many of the forces and trends in our current environment and identifies opportunities as well as challenges for social work.

Leach, R. 1993, *Political Ideologies* (2nd edn), Macmillan, Melbourne. Explores political ideologies in general and the Australian agenda.

Pakulski, J. 2004, *Globalising Inequalities: New patterns of social privilege and disadvantage*, Allen & Unwin, Sydney. A fascinating account of globalisation, its complexities and the new forms of inequalities it is producing at local, national and international levels.

Powell, F. 2001, *The Politics of Social Work*, Sage, London. This book addresses the implications of postmodernism for social work.

2
Context of professional practice

Phoebe Smith is a child protection worker with the department of children's services. Intense pressure from the public, the media and politicians on the issue of child sexual abuse, as well as the aftermath of a recent royal commission into police involvement in the protection of paedophilic networks, has seen a rapid growth in the numbers of cases of sexual abuse reported to the department. But the capacity of the department is limited, so a new set of guidelines has been established to determine which cases have priority. Shifting its resources to respond to the crisis has resulted in local departmental managers directing workers to 'flick' cases that do not have priority to local agencies in the non-government sector.

Phoebe has been working with one particular family for about three weeks. The family comprises Jill Williams, a 35-year-old divorcee, her 15-year-old daughter Karen, her 12-year-old son Bradley and Nigel, Jill's de facto partner who has been living with the family for some years. Terry Williams, Jill's ex-husband and the father of the two children, is also involved.

Initially the case was referred to the department by a school counsellor concerned about Bradley's behaviour. Both Karen and Bradley want to live with their father who, unfortunately, is not able to have them because his work keeps him away from town for long periods. Phoebe thinks that in Bradley's case he has not fully come to terms with his parents' break-up and divorce, although he seems to have a good relationship with Nigel. On the other hand, Karen's desire to move out is not so easily explicable. She is sullen and withdrawn and refuses to talk about her relationship with her mother or Nigel, or even what she thinks of Nigel. There is clearly something in the family dynamic that is causing Karen's withdrawal, but Phoebe cannot put her finger on it. She suspects there may be more to the relationship between Nigel and Karen but is reluctant to probe too deeply too quickly.

At the monthly case discussion with her manager, Phoebe is told she has spent too much time on the case already and is getting nowhere. Unless she can come up with some clear evidence of sexual abuse by Nigel, the manager tells her the case must be 'flicked' and the family recommended for counselling. Phoebe disagrees. She thinks that with more time she will get Karen to open up and reveal something. Phoebe berates her manager—she points out she was employed as a caseworker and must be allowed to exercise her professional skills, that other local agencies do not have the expertise to handle this type of case and, in any event, the department's policy of prioritising cases is at variance with the department's charter of service. She also asserts that the policy undermines her own professional ethics because it denies help to those in need.

The type of problem confronting Phoebe—the problem of scarce resources (her time, limited services, lack of expertise, etc.), and an organisation that seems to her to be driven by imperatives that conflict with her own professional ideals—is not unusual. In an ideal world of unlimited resources, Phoebe could devote as much time with the family as she believed was professionally justified, and her department would support her in that decision. She could get to the bottom of what is happening in the family and then bring to bear a range of other services and resources to protect those who are vulnerable and ameliorate the problems facing the family.

There is, however, another perspective on this and we must be careful in seeing conflict between professionals and their employing organisation in such stark terms. An organisation's policies and practices should not automatically be viewed as inimical to the needs and interests of the constituency it seeks to serve. Equally, we should be careful in accepting claims that professional norms or standards are the epitome of good practice. It would be naive to think it is a professional's, and for that matter an organisation's, ethical duty to meet all unmet needs, desirable though this might be. We also think, therefore, that some caution is required in accepting Rhodes' view that:

> human service organisations undermine our moral concepts, because of their contradictory nature: their stated goal is to help clients, yet their actual operation serves the interest of preserving the bureaucracy (Rhodes 1986:134).

Organisations can be accused of myriad failures, including being self-serving, but they also do a lot of other things as well. The issue is not that they erode moral responsibility, rather that they might offer alternative moralities to those subscribed to by professionals. Professions and professionals do not hold a monopoly on what constitutes the common weal or even what benefits their client group and it is an inescapable fact of modern professional life that choices must be made which create ethical conflicts for the worker.

Perhaps Phoebe has actually fallen into a trap that philosophers call 'the naturalistic fallacy'. This is when people confuse what is with what ought to be. Just because the department has traditionally undertaken long-term casework with vulnerable families, Phoebe believes that this is the ethically correct practice which she should defend, rather than consider that there might be alternatives. We say more about the naturalistic fallacy at the end of this chapter and in chapter 3.

In this chapter, we look in more detail at aspects of the 'agency-professional arena' identified by Payne (2005: 17). It is not our intention to dwell too much on the nature and purpose or theory of organisations because, for us, the more interesting question is the relationship between being a professional social worker in an organisation, and how the organisational context shapes and determines ethical practice. However, central to our discussion is the impact of the neo-liberal agenda, in the guise of 'new managerialism', that has had, and is having, a profound impact on the ways in which social services are delivered in many western capitalist countries.

We use the term 'organisation' to signify the range of social services in which a social worker may be employed. Rhodes uses the narrower term 'bureaucracy', which describes the particular form of organisational structure outlined by the German sociologist Max Weber (1864–1920) and is characterised by hierarchical authority, complex rules and regulations governing its activities, impersonal relations and specialised roles carried out by people employed for their technical expertise (Mouzelis 1975). While this is the form that dominates most social service delivery, it is by no means the only one. Other organisational forms—the collective, the cooperative and the community-managed organisation, for example—have emerged in recent years to address 'the perceived shortcomings of conventional [bureaucratic] structure' (Jones and May 1992: 219).

Notwithstanding that many of these 'alternative' forms of organisations claim to do many things better than the stereotypical public sector social service bureaucracy, they are not necessarily any better at preventing or dealing with some of the ethical problems faced by their workers. These organisations can be just as ideologically or politically driven in ways that might undermine the professional's service ethic or personal values. Professionals working in these types of organisations may be no less ethically challenged in their daily practice and no more able, in virtue of the organisational context, to resolve ethical conflicts when they arise.

Professional sphere

Despite one of the distinguishing features of social work being that it is almost exclusively carried out in an organisational context, Jones and

May observe that in the professional social work literature, how to work in organisations tends to be treated as a secondary, marginalised sphere of knowledge and skills (1992: 6–7). Indeed, precisely because social work is invariably carried out in an organisational context it is sometimes described as a 'bureau-profession or semi-profession' (Etzioni 1969). Whether social work is a profession is not our concern—we can leave that debate to the sociologists. We are assuming it is one because it shares the ethically relevant features of a profession.

Professions are those occupations that have as their explicit purpose the delivery of one or more basic goods that contribute to human flourishing (Oakley and Cocking 2001). According to these two authors the most important elements of professionalism are:

- adherence to a code of ethics or ethical standards,
- good judgement,
- client-centred practice,
- independence of thought or action, and
- competence.

As an ideal, professional practice in social service work involves the exercise of professional judgement and the application of specialised knowledge, skills and techniques in the achievement of some social purpose or end. We have noted that most social workers employ their professional repertoire in some kind or organisational setting, whether it is a government social service department or a non-government community-based, charitable or religious-based service. These may, to a greater or lesser degree, receive some financial support to carry out their activities from central or local government. With the exception of North America, there are few private, independent social work practitioners working on a 'fee-for-service' basis, in the same way there are lawyers, doctors or psychologists.

In addition to delivering social goods that contribute to human flourishing (Oakely and Cocking 2001, above), traditional definitions of professions also add that professions deliver these goods by the exercise of specialist knowledge or skills, and guarantee this expertise by the self-regulation of training, accreditation and professional standards (typically by way of codes of ethics, of which more will be discussed in chapter 4). Professions also use their codes and accreditation procedures to ensure that practitioners will continue to act on the morally important goals of the profession by offering guidance about how to act and, in many cases, deregistering and disbarring those who do not act appropriately.

In addition to education, self-regulation, and the exercise of autonomy or discretion in making judgements, autonomy in particular is taken to be essential for professionals because without it they would not be able to make decisions freely to act on their profession's special goals and would instead be forced to act on orders given by people (such as employers) or funding bodies outside the profession. Without autonomy the stated goals of a profession would largely be meaningless.

In chapter 1 we reported that the purpose or telos of social work, defined by the IFSW, is to promote 'social change, problem solving in human relationships and the empowerment and liberation of people to enhance well-being' (IFSW 2002), clearly a purpose that aims to improve human flourishing. With her concern for the Williams family, Phoebe, our caseworker, is implicitly working towards this aim. Two of her major concerns are that she is not being allowed to practise her professional skills nor to exercise autonomy. One of the challenges to social work identified in the last chapter as part of globalisation and the neo-liberal agenda is the trend to new managerialism.

The new managerialism

In last twenty years many western capitalist countries—the United Kingdom, Australia, New Zealand, Canada and the United States, to name a few—have embraced in some form or another, and to varying degrees, neo-liberal policies that involve sweeping and revolutionary changes to the public sector under the banners of 'new managerialism' and 'new public management'(Pollitt 1990; Considine 1994; Pusey 1991;

Hill 1997). The impact of these reforms have been profound (Kerr and Savelsberg 2001; see also Clarke and Newman 1997), particularly in the human services—health, education and social welfare services, for example—where private sector models of management, accounting and budgetary control, an emphasis on consumer choice overlaying values of accountability, efficiency and effectiveness, coupled with measurable outcomes or throughputs, have been central to these reforms.

Nicholas Deakin, commenting on the UK's public sector reforms and new managerialism, identified nine key characteristics: the disaggregation of services; competition; management styles borrowed from the private sector; parsimony in resource use; a shift to procedural rules away from discretion; a results or outcomes focus; a 'hands-on' management approach; measurable performance standards; and control by output measures (Deakin 1999: 180). Similar characteristics can be observed in other countries, such as Australia (Pusey 1991; Considine 1994).

A central feature of the new public sector management has been the application of private sector models to traditional human service delivery. One such model is increased control over workers and the way they work, achieved through a range of strategies such as:

> routinising and measuring work loads, staff reward systems, reducing job security, removing or redeploying staff, 'casualising' the workforce, dissolving 'bureaucratic rigidities' in the employment relationship, reducing unionisation, weakening industrial awards, and creating small and separate work units (Nabben 2001).

Furthermore, because business decisions are fundamentally guided by clear, quantifiable, short-term profit measures, the same types of measures are given to public sector programs and the emphasis now is on customers and consumer choice, competitors, products, throughput and efficiencies (Nabben 2001). Child protection services, interestingly, have become one of the sites over which managerialist policies and practices have been introduced and overlaid. Child protection practice has become proceduralised through the imposition of guidelines and standards contained in departmental manuals to the point where workers 'working by the book' now spend more time investigating allegations than they do working with families and children (Banks 2001; Parton et al. 1997; Parton and Byrne 2000).

Van den Broek's study (2003) of the NSW Childline service—a call centre system designed to centralise all child-at-risk reports throughout the state, including after hours—is particularly instructive, not least because it forced workers to change the way they carried out their work. The intention of the Childline service was to:

> broaden the scope and increase access to [child protection] services, increase public awareness of the service, and extend and facilitate new mandatory reporting guidelines. Specifically, it was expected to increase the quality, consistency, equity and responsiveness of [child protection] services, deliver customer friendly service, refocus general enquiries and intake processes in a centralised system, and free up [child protection] frontline staff to increase face-to-face time with children and their families (2003: 241).

Notwithstanding its stated aims, Childline adopted a classic 'low road' call centre model focusing on quantitative statistics through the use of display boards detailing factors such as call waiting time, number of calls in the queue and the number of staff members taking calls (van den Broek 2003: 244). Crucially, caseworkers complained they were being deskilled because of the ways tasks were fragmented and routinised. Moreover, caseworkers felt they were unable to use and build practice-relevant knowledge or to reflect on and utilise contextual information critically and creatively. Workers were expected to complete case reports in the recommended time of twenty minutes when, in many cases, workers stated they needed more time because of the seriousness and complexity of the cases they had to deal with (2003: 244–6).

The ascendancy and dominance of the managerialist approach, while obviously influencing the nature of professional social work, is not all doom and gloom and it is doubtful if the neo-liberal enterprise could ever be truly successful in imposing private sector models on human services for two main reasons. In the first place, private sector businesses are accountable to their shareholders; public and non-government social services serve, and are accountable to, more than just the immediate constituency they are established to serve. Second, they have to reconcile a range of competing interests and their role is often 'embedded in politically complex public problems, where solutions can often only be achieved through collaboration between a range of interdependent services' (Nabben 2001: 44). Crucially, however, the private sector managerialist model is unable to capture the complexities of the human services and the kinds of problems they are dealing with and seeking to ameliorate.

Hasenfeld and English (cited in Donovan and Jackson 1991: 18) summarise some of these complexities that mean new managerialism cannot be translated successfully into the human services. These include:

- The raw material of human services is human beings.
- Goal definition . . . is problematical and ambiguous.
- The technology . . . is indeterminate.
- Staff-client relations are the core activity.
- Human services lack reliable and valid measures of effectiveness.

In addition, the obvious problem is that new managerialism is fundamentally about improving profit margins or being more cost-effective. In comparison, human services are essentially about improving human wellbeing. Because of the difficulties of measuring the effectiveness of improving human wellbeing, it may be that new managerialism has led to a reduction of quality, where programs are getting cheaper but producing worse results (Donovan and Jackson 1991). The irony is that these difficulties actually provide social workers with the opportunities to use the systems and processes in more creative ways—the idea of 'working with' the context that we introduced in the last chapter. This puts considerable onus on human service workers to become critically reflective professionals, able to engage with policy debates, remind decision-makers about the fundamental purposes of human services and reintroduce the ethical dimension. What our caseworker Phoebe is experiencing is an ethical conflict between her professional goals and the requirements of the organisation.

Ethical conflict and the organisation

Ethical conflict is inevitable in circumstances where social workers need to make decisions and exercise their professional judgement. Hirschman (1970) was one of the first to describe organisational conflict and resolution through the concepts of 'exit' and 'voice'. According to Hirschman, action related to these issues can be clustered around three types:

- do nothing/passive acceptance,
- speak up/seek change, and
- exit/resign (in this latter case, the exit of workers may bring about change, but that is not usually the principal purpose of this type of action).

Responses to organisational conflict can be mapped two-dimensionally as in Figure 1 (adapted from Keeley and Graham 1991: 350–1).

Unfortunately, there may well be circumstances where the worker feels the level of conflict is irresolvable and the only course of action is to exit the organisation. The type of activity that is manifested in vociferous exit (Cell 2) usually involves resignation in protest, but might also include whistleblowing, industrial action or some other kind of public agitation that may or may not effect change in time. Whistleblowing is, as De Maria (1997) observes, inherently individualistic and often comes at great personal and professional cost to the worker as she or he feel they have no other course of action.

Figure 2.1: Exit and voice

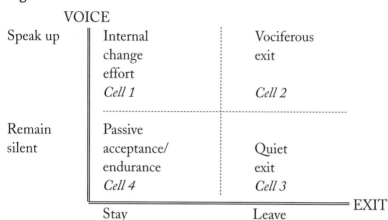

Figure adapted from 'Exit Voice and Ethics', 1991 *Journal of Business Ethics*, vol. 10, p. 350.

Remaining in Cell 4, where the professional stays but does nothing, comes also with personal and professional costs—by definition it often results in job neglect, discontent and an undermining of the worker's professional ethos. An example of this is the professional who tolerates organisational policies that undermine the dignity and autonomy of their clients and does not seek ways of getting those policies changed. Such workers fail themselves professionally and personally, as well as their clients, the organisation and, ultimately, the wider community.

Cell 1 should represent the ultimate expression of voice in an organisational context—positive manifestations of change and improvement of benefit to the clients or constituency served by the organisation, and the organisation itself. Within that quadrant what is sought is congruence between professional and organisational values in ways that are professionally satisfying to the worker.

It is in Cell 1 that we locate our ideas about ethical practice and where we see workers as ethically articulate activists for change. Although some workers may ultimately have to exit an organisation on matters of moral conscience, it is our view that workers must, in the first instance, exercise their ethical voice. Those workers we spoke about in the introduction who, for one reason or another, had chosen not to take up the challenge and seek change in their practice environment are undermining and diminishing their professional project.

By definition, ethical practice is concerned with change and for that to occur we must have an ethically articulate profession that is able to exercise its collective ethical voice. It is not our intention in this book to spell out the myriad ways in which workers can challenge and change their practice environment. Rather our aim is to encourage the development of an ethical vocabulary as part of any change process. An essential element in this vocabulary is the idea of 'ethical satisficing' in the context of 'bounded ethical practice'. We examine these ideas in the following section.

Bounded ethical decision-making

Ethical practice is concerned with making decisions or judgements about how to act or what to do, and being able to justify those actions and behaviours within some kind of philosophical framework. Ethical dilemmas often take one of two forms. First, some evidence suggests that to do act X is morally right (maintaining confidentiality), but other evidence suggests that to do act Y is morally wrong (keeping a secret that results in harm to someone). If the evidence in either case is inconclusive then our anxiety about what we should do is compounded. The second common situation is where a person believes that, on moral grounds, she or he both ought to and ought not to perform act X; for example, in the case of withdrawing life support for a permanently comatose person (Beauchamp and Childress 1989: 5). These are cases of moral dilemmas, situations where ethical reasons do not readily determine a single course of action.

The lucky among us, guided by unreflective certitude, may know exactly what they would do in such cases and do it unquestioningly. For the rest of us, these ethical dilemmas are of a type we might regularly face, and where we could choose either option and still feel uncomfortable and dissatisfied. In an organisational context, our private, inner ethical conflict takes on an added dimension when it becomes an open disagreement with colleagues, clients or our organisation.

When faced with ethical dilemmas, many workers—particularly new workers—approach the problem as if they can be simply and immediately resolved by applying some kind of ethical formula with varying degrees of sophistication, as if all ethical problems have nice neat outcomes. Regrettably, this view is often reinforced in books on practical ethics and we would contend that this engenders much of the ethical discontent among practitioners when things do not fit into the formula.

In the real-world swamp of practice, and particularly in the organisational context of social work, nothing is that simple. Our approach in this text is that ethics is necessarily pragmatic—we are not aiming for the perfect decision or outcome, but the best that can be achieved in the circumstances. The context for this approach is what we term 'bounded ethical practice', which is our attempt to paint a more realistic picture of social work practice.

The idea of bounded ethical practice or bounded ethical decision-making draws on Herbert Simon's influential *Administrative Behaviour*, first published in 1945 (Simon 1976). There, and in later work, he argued that decision-making within organisations has its basis in what he calls 'bounded rationality'. In Simon's view, bounded rationality happens because decision-makers can never know with any certainty if what they decide is optimal or maximal. So, within the limits of their situation, decision-makers can only 'satisfice'—make decisions that are more or less good or right.

Despite some limitations with Simon's psychological conception of the rational person, the idea of bounded rationality and the process of 'satisficing' offers an important insight about decision-making and ethical practice within social service work. Bounded ethical practice arises because of the complex and multi-dimensional context of practice. Practitioners satisfice in their ethical practice, not because of some inherent defect in their moral character but because their practice environment demands it. Bounded ethical practice thus involves a constant process of reconciliation, negotiation and redefinition of the ever-present conflicting values in social service work to reach an equilibrium that satisfies the needs of clients, the organisation, law and policy, the worker, colleagues and, ultimately, the community at large.

The ethical satisficer reduces the complexities of the practice environment to a realistically manageable level by choosing those alternatives that meet his or her basic expectations and aspirations. The decisions they make or the resolutions they come to in the event of conflict are not necessarily ideal, but they ought to be the best in the circumstances and they ought to be ones the worker can, in good conscience, live with. The alternative is for the worker to burn themselves out in their fight against colleagues, their employing organisation and others as they constantly search for their utopian vision of ethical perfection.

Having said that, ethical satisficing does not necessarily imply a minimalist conception of good practice, although undoubtedly this is an accurate assessment of what often has to happen. Nevertheless, the process of satisficing may mean that levels of aspiration are adjusted downwards until 'goals reach levels that are practically attainable' (March and Simon 1958: 151). Reaching this understanding is important in our conception of ethical practice.

In the short term, Phoebe may have to adjust her ethical aspirations downwards in relation to the Williams family, although there are some strategies she can adopt. She can't just rail at her bosses in meetings in instinctive reaction to perceived injustice. Instead she needs to reflect seriously on the policies, discuss the issues with her colleagues, gain support and consider a range of views, take into account the way decisions are made within the organisation and work with these structures to bring as many players on side as she can. There may be a number of options she should consider apart from doing the work herself. However, she can put her supervisor on notice that the matter is not closed. The least she can do is to gather information about what resources for the Williams family are available outside the department and make sure that if she can't support them someone else can.

Phoebe needs an ethical vocabulary to frame the issue in terms that allow the organisation to respond to the problem more appropriately and effectively. She needs to understand that the organisation faces its own ethical dilemma about resource allocation and how it is going to satisfy its service charter. It is not just Phoebe's problem; it is also the organisation's. If Phoebe is permitted to spend a great deal of time on one family, others will miss out on any service. There are two equally justifiable ethical positions here—it is not necessarily the case that the individual practitioner is 'right' and the organisation 'wrong'.

Virtues

The virtue of open-mindedness that we introduced in chapter 1 is important if Phoebe is to be able to see all sides of the question. Open-mindedness is a foundation for the virtue we introduce in this chapter: being able to exercise good judgement, also called practical reasoning. This may not seem like a virtue at first glance, but more like a skill. As we stated in the introduction the three themes can overlap, and this one clearly involves a knowledge of critical reasoning and skills in analysis. However, the capacity for practical reasoning also requires important elements of character, elements that take discipline and practice to develop. In Phoebe's case her single-minded pursuit of her client's welfare as she sees it may be admirable, but has also led her to make a rapid, even one-sided judgement. This judgement, coupled with her enthusiasm, has led in turn to heightened conflict within the workplace. The possibility of a well-reasoned, all-things-considered decision requires a degree of detachment, imagination and the sort of active listening skills that should be a part of social workers' basic skills. This capacity for calm reflection is not the same as the virtue of reasonableness, which is a willingness to compromise, but clearly many apparent conflicts will be resolved by compromise once all aspects of a situation are better understood.

The capacity for practical reasoning can be deliberately developed. Classroom debates and other formal exercises in debate are excellent tools for this. These exercises provide a safe environment in which it is easier to recognise and look closer at alternative points of view. The various study tasks in this book provide possible bases for these sorts of debates and thus help develop ethical capacities as well as ethical knowledge.

Ethical skills

In chapter 1 we introduced the idea of validity in arguments. In this chapter we are going to look again at the final argument we presented there:

> Major premise: All social workers drink heavily at the pub on Friday afternoons
> Minor premise: Mikaela is a social worker
> Conclusion: Mikaela drinks heavily at the pub on Friday afternoons

This is a valid argument because if the major premise is true and the minor premise is true then the conclusion must be true. This example differs in structure from the earlier, invalid example involving Donald who may be a duck, because the minor premise links Mikaela to the major premise as a member of the class, not because she shares the same property. Connecting the minor premise to the right part of the major premise is crucial to validity.

If you knew that the premises were true you could rely on the conclusion. Unfortunately that's a big if. In fact the major premise is false because only some social workers drink heavily. It only takes one social worker who doesn't drink to render the major premise false.

The argument is valid, but it is not sound. A sound argument is one with a valid structure *and* true premises. Validity by itself proves nothing. Soundness depends upon knowledge of relevant facts. This is what army and management types have taken to calling 'situational awareness'. The successful ethical worker will therefore have to be someone who has all the relevant facts before reaching a decision. This situational awareness has two distinct elements. First, you need to learn how to do research. If you are at university or college right now, this is a perfect time to acquire these skills.

The other aspect is the capacity to understand your workplace. The discussion of the agency and professional contexts of your work serves us well here, as it reinforces the need to exercise good interpersonal skills and 'organisational competence'. This will also be important when using inductive methods to predict future results of current decisions, an important aspect of consequentialist ethical decision-making (see chapter 3).

The rules governing validity and soundness offer formal reasons for objecting to an argument. In particular, you can check to see if the premises really do entail (necessarily lead to) the conclusion, and to see if unwarranted assumptions have been made about contestable facts. There are also informal objections you can raise, which are covered in the next chapter under the heading of fallacies.

At another level, being able to apply a number of skills would have helped Phoebe. If she had a greater awareness of the way in which the political discourse shapes the delivery of services, she may have been in a position to better evaluate what was occurring and apply her understanding to the way in which the political discourse shapes the department's child protection services. This in turn would have empowered her to develop a more informed response. However, this means she needs to have as much regard to what informs her agency's policies and procedures as she does of the theory that guides the assessment of families. Phoebe's understanding of her profession and her ethical responsibilities relative to her responsibilities as an employee also need further development if conflicts such as she is experiencing are to be resolved.

Ethical knowledge

The key piece of ethical knowledge from this chapter is the notion of satisficing. This comes from integrating the identified virtues and skills discussed above. Exercising and applying knowledge can be far more difficult than acquiring it. Weighing up the options and choosing the best one for the circumstances comes from practice experience and, for Phoebe, stresses the need for her to liaise with more experienced colleagues. Perhaps if Phoebe had discussed the management of the Williams family, the related departmental policies and what her code had to say about her responsibilities to her employer with more experienced colleagues before she met with her manager, she may have been more informed. This would have meant she was better able to think and act strategically. This in turn would have saved her a lot of distress and she could have been a more effective advocate for the Williams children.

Conclusion

The idea that social workers are radically disempowered is at the heart of most 'postmodern' critiques of social work. The postmodern context of contemporary social work is thought by many to entrench relative powerlessness. Bureaucratism, managerialism and features of globalisation serve to make grass roots action, individual and community self-determination and professional independence much harder, if not impossible. This context may well present fresh challenges or sharpen existing challenges, but there is no need to assume that this means we need to accept the situation as necessary, even if we accept that the situation really is as bad as the postmodern theorists say it is.

These criticisms have some real teeth, but ultimately they oversimplify the complexities of social work practice. The distinction between the observation of existing states of affairs, and the theorising of better ones, is what ethics is all about. If we fall for the 'naturalistic fallacy' (the belief that what has happened is inevitable or good) then we will never have any motivation to engage in ethical inquiry or work for change. But it is a fallacy. There is no good reason to think that social work must be disempowering just because it often is. Provided we can describe a better alternative, and have reason to think the alternative would work, then we have a reason, maybe even an obligation, to seek to change things.

The basis of much of the ethical conflict in organisational contexts revolves around the defence of professional autonomy. As Phoebe's situation demonstrates, the idea of professional autonomy sits very uneasily within an organisational and political framework. Besides being subject to internal organisational rules and regulations that may limit, control or sometimes proscribe certain professional choices and judgements, practitioners must also exercise their professional judgement according to broader policy directions, determined ultimately by government and mediated through the organisation. This is certainly true of workers in statutory agencies, and it is becoming more so for the non-government welfare sector which is increasingly controlled through tied funding grants linked to the pre-determined policy directions of government.

Jones and May (1992) suggest that enhancing and protecting autonomy involves developing a strong political base in the organisation from which to influence both policy and practice. Political power is, they argue, bound up with legitimacy that stems from such things as:

> prestige of the profession . . . their perceived competence and track record, personal prestige, and the clarity of the workers' mandate to perform organisational tasks and responsibilities (1992: 287).

Jones and May also stress the importance of using the professionalism of social work and social welfare strategically, and this includes using their professional and industrial associations. One of the key resources that workers have in asserting their professionalism, but which is often largely under-utilised, is their code of ethics. While it is often easy to dismiss ethical codes as part of the professionalising repertoire of occupations seeking to carve out occupational space in the human services or to assert their irrelevance because of their generality and vagueness—guidelines without lines to guide (Collingridge 1995)—codes can, often in conjunction with an organisation's own charter, customer code, principles of practice or whatever, provide a very important and useful tool for the practitioner to contest the ethical terrain. We say more about the function and value of codes in chapter 4.

Study tasks

1   Consider the case study at the beginning of this chapter. Do you think that Phoebe had strong ethical grounds for her position? Argue your case, giving reasons for and against.
2   Think about an organisation in which you have had some experience either as a worker, volunteer, student or client. Can you locate employees' actions in the four cells identified by Hirschman?
3   Have you experienced anyone who has taken a position similar to that represented in Cell 1? What happened and were they effective? Discuss with someone else who is interested in ethics.
4   What is your reaction to the ideas of 'bounded ethical practice' and 'satisficing'? Are these really a sell-out for ethical activists?

Further reading

Banks, S. 2001, *Ethics and Values in Social Work* (2nd edn), Palgrave Macmillan, Basingstoke, Hampshire, esp. chapter 7 'Social Workers' Duties: Policies, procedures and the new managerialism'. A good introduction to the conflicting duties facing social workers in organisations taking on the 'new managerialism' and 'new authoritarianism'. Banks' discussion of reflective versus defensive practice in this context is particularly useful.

Banks, S. 2004, *Ethics, Accountability and the Social Professions*, Palgrave Macmillan, Basingstoke. This excellent book explores the nature of professions, professionalism and the place of the 'social professions' in relation to ethics. It is an important extension of the introductory discussion on the nature of professionalism offered in this chapter.

Kultgen, J. 1988, *Ethics and Professionalism*, University of Pennsylvania Press, Philadelphia. A bitingly critical view of the professions and how ethics can be twisted into a self-serving tool to increase professional power and control.

Oakley, J. and Cocking, D. 2001, *Virtue Ethics and Professional Roles*, Cambridge University Press, Cambridge.

Sinclair, A. 1996, 'Codes in the Workplace: Organisational versus professional codes' in M. Coady and S. Bloch (eds), *Codes of Ethics and the Professions*, Melbourne University Press, Melbourne, pp. 88–108. This chapter explores the promise and limits of organisational codes of ethics, and compares their functions to professional codes of ethics. A good introduction to thinking about ethics in the organisational context.

Sullivan, W.M. 2004, *Work and Integrity: The Crisis and Promise of Professionalism in America*, Jossey-Bass, San Francisco, California. Discusses the role of professions and the connection between this idea and ethical practice.

3
What ethics?

Cara* worked in a counselling service catering to homeless young people in a large Australian city. One day two detectives from the homicide squad came to see her. They wanted to ask her about one of her clients, a young man with a history of violence, petty crime and drug abuse. They stated that he might somehow be involved in a recent murder and wanted to ask Cara some questions about his state of mind, drug use and relationship with the victim. Cara was uncomfortable talking about her client with outsiders and said that she would have to speak to her supervisor. The police officers became agitated, even aggressive. They suggested that her unwillingness to cooperate with their inquiries would amount to obstruction, and perhaps even an attempt to pervert the course of justice. Cara felt as if she had been threatened with arrest. Despite her better judgement Cara gave them an interview and the police went away satisfied.

Distressed by the incident and in need of some guidance, Cara went to her supervisor and retold the story. Far from being sympathetic, her supervisor became angry and accused Cara of breaching client confidentiality and flagrantly disregarding the organisation's code of practice. Cara was sacked for these

_____

* This is a true story but Cara's name has been changed to protect her identity.

offences and left her job feeling bitter and very confused about what, if anything, she could have done to avoid getting into trouble.

Cara's case is not unusual, even if the result of what happened to her was extreme. Social workers are often caught in ethical binds. Cara felt unable to resist the pressure brought to bear by the detectives, and equally unable to prevent the retribution meted out by her boss. In deciding whether or not to talk to the police Cara faced a serious dilemma: should she cooperate with the inquiry, acting on a possible legal, certainly a moral, obligation to help the police solve serious crimes, or should she refuse, thus acting on an organisational and professional duty to maintain client confidentiality? These sorts of dilemmas arise largely because of the position social workers occupy within organisations and institutions.

This chapter is concerned with the idea of ethics. What does the term mean? How can the formal study of ethics improve the delivery and efficacy of professional social work services?

Cara's case is useful to understanding these issues because it revolves around a dilemma. A dilemma is a moral challenge involving a choice between two options (or perhaps more), when there are strong reasons to do both things or not to do them. The outcome is that, whatever choice is made, it will result in some other important moral failing (such as failing in some duty, failing to avoid some bad outcome or failing to honour an important commitment or relationship). These situations have a clear structure, and so a study of the nature of our commitments and of the processes of formal decision-making is enormously helpful.

Resolving Cara's situation requires a critical eye being run over her obligations, looking at the political, social and organisational contexts in which they arise to decide what her various duties are, and how much weight to attach to them. It is also necessary to know what options she and her manager had, whether any of her duties were outweighed by the consequences (good or bad) of those options, and whether any of these choices were incompatible with her professional or personal integrity.

Deciding these things in turn requires understanding what values Cara has as a person and as a social worker, where they come from and how they give rise to particular principles upon which she can act. On the face of it, a decision like this is complex, even overwhelming.

It will help to begin at the beginning. Just what do we mean by 'ethics'?

What is ethics?

The study of ethics can be obscure to the uninitiated. This is largely because today the words 'ethics' and 'morality' are often used interchangeably. When confronted with the suggestion that you should study ethics it is therefore natural to think that you are being asked to learn how to be good. Nothing could be further from the truth. In fact ethics and morality, while related, have very different meanings.

Ethics has its origins in the ancient Greek word *ethikos*, which means the theory of living well. The study of ethics was originally the study of how people could live so as to be successful, happy and flourishing. The emphasis was on the 'good life'. Only later, in the thinking of Roman philosophers, did the emphasis shift to the 'good person'. The Romans gave us the word 'morality' from the Latin *mos* or custom. (This is the same root from which we get 'mores'.) From the ancient Greek thinkers Socrates and Plato we get the idea that these two are related. Socrates in particular felt that justice and fulfilment of one's obligations was a part of ethics because he thought unjust people were ultimately degraded and unhappy people who could not fulfil their higher nature or purpose. Morality is therefore nestled inside the wider scope of ethics, much like a yoke within an egg.

Today ethics is still considered to be the study of an art or skill. Just as it was for the Greeks, ethics remains an intensely practical matter. Despite having a firm grasp of moral duty and being properly motivated to do what is right, a good person will struggle to define just what it takes to be a good social worker. Leaving fundamental moral principles to the counsel of your own conscience, we will look at the commitments of the social work profession, and how the techniques of formal ethics can help a well-motivated person to figure out what they ought to do in difficult or novel situations. In particular we are interested in the unique problems that arise in professional contexts, problems that cannot be resolved by reference to ordinary moral principles. The study of dilemmas and other problems is useful in itself. You will encounter plenty of these in your professional life and it will be helpful to have some strategies to respond to them. However these cases also help to better understand the general principles and values that guide empowered social work.

In this book we will often use the terms 'values' and 'principles'. These ethical concepts help us to make practical use of the distinction between morality and ethics, but they represent a slightly different though related distinction. Values belong to the sphere of morality in that they involve judgements about good and bad, better and worse, and the ideals we strive towards. Most moral judgements are either decisions concerning what values to have, or expressions of our values.

When we talk about values in this book, we are not concerned with the deeply personal judgements and beliefs that provide individual practitioners with their moral compass. These sorts of values are beyond the scope of formal ethics, but they are vital to the individual's ethical conduct. We are concerned with the shared values that the social work profession develops, and to which people commit when they become social workers. These kinds of values are not so deeply personal, and they tend to arise from more explicit processes of reflection and dialogue. They are still values in the sense that they tell us what standards we aspire to, what ideals we use to guide practice and what we think of as good in social work.

Principles are guides to action that put our values into practice. They are not the same as values, because they tell us what to do in certain defined situations. In this way they belong to the action-guiding domain of ethics. Values will tell us what is good or what to aim to achieve, but they do not by themselves tell us what to do in each situation. A number of principles may develop from a single value. For example, many people value the dignity of individuals. When guided by this value, a person might adopt a principle of non-interference, and another principle of actively helping people in trouble (beneficence). In some circumstances effect is given to our values by allowing other people to make their own decisions (autonomy), while in different circumstances effect is given to the same value by intervention (paternalism). These might seem like contradictory ideas, but in fact what matters are the circumstances or context.

The relationship between values and principles helps us to understand what connects morality to the broader domain of ethics. Values give guidance, and a sense of right and wrong. However it is frequently not clear how to act on personal and professional values, and so it is necessary to look to the specifics of each situation, to various rules and other factors to decide what is required. Practical judgement isn't completely divorced from moral beliefs, but the context of action means that we cannot simply be guided directly by our moral beliefs. Often, people with different beliefs will still have reasons to accept the same principles, allowing people from diverse backgrounds to work together in professional settings. Conversely, people will often find that in the wider world they need to respond to the needs and interests of others, to accommodate the different values of others, and to take the equal worth of others into account. All of these factors provide additional reasons for acting, reasons that can often modify or even sometimes cancel out the reasons provided by your most basic moral beliefs. This is why there is a serious obligation to justify or explain your actions, because this is how you show others that you have taken their views and beliefs into account.

Three modes of ethical thinking

There are a number of modes of ethical thinking that reflect different ethical theories. The perspective of ethics employed in this work is built upon a particular view of the relationship between these approaches.

The first point is that we regard all the standard approaches to ethics as modes, not distinct and competing schools or theories. Ethics is a practical matter and cannot be reduced to the pleasing elegance of a simple theory based on a single principle or value. Instead, complex real-world problems demand subtle and flexible approaches. All of the traditional approaches capture some aspect of the truth of ethical complexity, and all of them, if properly balanced, contribute to success-ful resolutions of real problems. The approach we advocate involves developing strategies that will enable the competent professional to deploy all the tools of ethics to deal with challenges as they arise.

The three major approaches or modes of ethics are virtue-based, deontology or duty-based and consequentialism.

Virtue-based ethics

Virtue is another name for good character. People are judged to have a good character by how they act, so in this way the theory explains both what values each person should have and what principles should guide their actions.

This is an ancient approach, originating with the ancient Greek ethicist Aristotle, who argued that all things have an end or *telos* towards which they move and against which they are measured. We discussed teleology in the knowledge theme of chapter 1. Teleology is not, strictly speaking, an ethical modality; however, Aristotle used his teleological method to develop a theory of virtue ethics. A virtue ethics is one that concentrates upon the character of the person doing the acting. As a result it concentrates upon finding ways to help people develop those character traits, such as generosity, courage, prudence and practical wisdom that help a person to live well. These individual positive charac-ter traits are called virtues. Traits, like sloth or greed that tend to make people worse off and unhappy, are called vices.

In many ways our approach to ethical practice is a virtue approach, because we are trying to advance arguments in favour of doing social work in a particular way and in favour of developing certain traits such as moral courage and activism. However, ours is not a pure virtue ethics approach because we do not believe that virtue ethics stands alone as a theory. Social work requires independent arguments to establish what its purpose is, and it cannot be successfully carried on without clear rules and principles. Nevertheless virtue ethics remains the central modality of our approach because we think the good social worker will not be a blind rule-follower. In fact, they will use good judgement (practical wisdom) to decide when to break rules if necessary (an exercise of the virtue of moral courage).

Deontological or duty-based ethics

Deontology concentrates on the inherent qualities of an action, largely judged by whether an action is in accordance with universal moral rules. Sometimes deontological theories include a firm list of universal rules. In other cases deontologists concentrate on explaining how to figure out what rules to adopt, depending on the various features of the situation we all face.

Immanuel Kant, the godfather of deontology, thought that a system he called the 'categorical imperative' could produce rules for any situation. In its simplest form the categorical imperative says that each of us should always act in such a way that our actions could become a rule for everyone without creating a contradiction. For example, if you want to lie in a particular situation you should assume that if you lie then everyone else will start lying too. But if this happened, then lying itself would be impossible because lying depends on trust. If everyone lied then no one would ever believe what anyone said and lying would not work. Successful lying requires other people to keep telling the truth. It involves the liar treating themselves as an exception, which violates what Kant thought of as a fundamental obligation, to treat all people as morally equal, a principle that social workers adopt under the banner of equal dignity and worth.

Following Kant, modern deontologists talk in terms of 'duty'. From a study of duties or obligations at the meta-ethical level, these moral philosophers derive rules of conduct at the normative level (that is, rules that tell each person how they should behave). One major controversy in 'pure' deontology involves the problem of deciding what to do when two or more rules conflict. These conflicts or dilemmas are difficult for deontologists to resolve. Duties don't cancel themselves out simply because they are in conflict—they remain important in social work practice. What is needed is a way to resolve the conflict, and deontology alone does not provide this. When you take into account different ethical modes you gain fresh perspectives and alternative ways of resolving such conflicts more successfully.

In this book we concentrate upon the rules and obligations that arise in the context of social work. These are special rules that are dependent on the unique professional context of the work, so we call these context-dependent rules. It does not matter if you do or don't think deontology is a generally sound ethical system, or believe that there are universal moral laws. It is clear that the context of social work practice creates rules that apply to you because you are a social worker. We call this perspective 'normative pluralism' partly because the insights of one mode or theory often cross over into others. Teleology is normally thought to be part of virtue ethics, but it also helps us to understand context-dependent deontological rules, because in working out what rules should structure and guide social work ethics we must refer to the goals and aims of social work. Also, as Kant himself made clear, the good deontological agent must also possess certain virtues, which he called the 'good will', a willingness to do what is right and a desire to live morally.

Consequentialism

Another major ethical perspective is consequentialism. In consequentialist modes of thinking what matters are outcomes. The most famous form of this approach is called 'utilitarianism'. It was first developed by the

Englishman Jeremy Bentham in the late eighteenth and early nineteenth centuries. His approach, known as hedonism, is based on the psychological idea that people are primarily motivated by the seeking of pleasure and the avoidance of pain. To Bentham all sources of pleasure and pain are equal, morally speaking. What is good is the maximum amount of pleasure or happiness and the minimum possible amount of pain or unhappiness, added up across all those people affected. The right action in any situation is the one that will achieve the best or most utilitarian outcome.

Many people make the mistake of thinking that an action will be judged by its actual outcomes. Because no one can know for sure what will happen at the time when they act, students and critics alike have thought that consequentialism must be false. Is it fair to judge an action as right or wrong because of its consequences if the consequences are unknown? Isn't it unfair to force people to act without knowing if they will be judged to have acted well or badly later on, depending on outcomes they can't fully control? However, consequentialist ethics rely only on the outcomes that can be reasonably foreseen. If a person acts thoughtlessly or recklessly then they can be held accountable for the unforeseen results they ought to have realised would happen. Generally, however, each person acts in anticipation of the expected results given the known features of the situation, past experience and so on. If something happens that nobody could reasonably have expected then this is what is called bad moral luck. Some social work ethicists think that social workers cannot be held accountable for such bad luck, while others think that, while it is tragic, social workers must shoulder responsibility for such events. The argument is that if their actions contribute to bad outcomes then they should feel responsible or else they will be callous and inclined to shelter behind their bureaucratic personas to distance themselves from their clients (Hollis and Howe 1987).

Bentham's relatively crude approach was refined by John Stuart Mill, the son of one of Bentham's disciples. He combined Bentham's utilitarianism with an Aristotelian concern for the good life and flourishing, and a Kantian concern for the equal moral value of all individual persons. From this method he developed the earliest clear formulation of modern liberalism, especially in his famous work *On Liberty* (1987, originally published in 1859). This approach, which emphasises the rights of individuals and the limits of legitimate governmental power, has become a cornerstone of modern democratic theory. Rights have become almost the sole modality of modern ethics in the West, and often seem mysterious. In Mill's version, rights are not strange metaphysical absolutes, but a way of regulating the relationship between the individual and the state or society. The moral value of the individual is protected by laws and moral rules that limit what society can do in the name of the common good. In other words, rights are simply mechanisms created to balance concern for consequences with the deontologist's concern for the moral equality of individuals.

Both consequentialist and deontological or duty-based approaches to ethics are informed by a 'liberal' philosophy, a term these days that can be quite confusing because it is used to mean both the concern for balancing individual rights and the greater good and, in some countries, it can also refer to someone who is left wing. Especially in America, the word is often used to mean someone with a distinct social agenda. People also use related terms such as 'libertarian' (meaning someone who thinks that individual rights are absolute and society has no right to limit or control individuals) and neo-liberal. It is important not to get these terms confused. In this book, when we use the term 'liberal' we mean the ethical position that seeks to balance individual rights and the common good, a view compatible with the pluralism of our ethical approach. We also talk about neo-liberalism, by which we mean the political and economic view that government should take little or no role in the promotion of social policies.

Both of these approaches (consequentialism and duty-based or deontological) matter in complex ethical thinking. Generally well-founded rules will promote values central to social work practice, while all actions can and should be judged by their expected benefit for all involved. Consequentialism is particularly important in social work ethics because most of what is done is designed or intended to have positive effects, and to take us closer to our goal or telos.

In short, the approach of this book can be described as 'pluralism', the view that in ethics a variety of ethical modes must be used to reach well-balanced, all things considered, judgements. There are two varieties of this pluralism employed in this book: value and normative. Value pluralism is the acceptance that people have a wide diversity of basic moral views. We believe that this diversity need not stop social workers sharing ethical viewpoints, because the telos of social work itself will give us reasons for the principles social workers collectively act on. Much of the rest of this book develops shared values and principles. The method of decision-making that uses all the modes of ethical reason can be called normative pluralism. In chapter 9 we will look more closely at how such pluralistic decisions can be achieved.

Ethics in social work

The ethics of social welfare practice is a part of what has come to be known as 'professional ethics'. Professional ethics, which can also be called 'vocational ethics', is not the study of what makes for a 'good' or successful person, but what makes a good professional. We will be attempting to answer the question, 'What makes a good social worker?' The first step is to understand what the word 'good' means in this context.

All varieties of professional ethics concentrate upon improving practice. This implies a standard or goal towards which each of us is always moving and against which our current state can be measured. This ideal state (reborn in modern management-speak under the name 'best practice') is what should be aimed for. 'Good' therefore means 'not best' (this is probably impossible) but 'sufficient for success'. This is the everyday sense of good, as in 'this is a good hammer', not the moral sense of good as in well behaved or compliant with duty. This is why we think virtue ethics and the teleological method are so important for professional ethics, because to the extent that if professional ethics is about more than ordinary ethics it is about the practicalities of doing the job well.

Virtues

The third of the virtues we wish to add to our profile of the good social worker is moral courage. Courage is one of the favourite examples of classical philosophers, but this has traditionally been equated with physical courage. However, when someone confronts a difficult situation such as Cara does in our case study, they must draw on fairly deep resources to hold their ground under such intense pressure.

The example of courage illustrates how Aristotle conceives of virtues. Since the early use of virtue theory by Roman Christian philosophers like St Augustine we have become accustomed to think of a virtue as the opposite of a vice. So courage is naturally thought to be the opposite of cowardice. Aristotle saw virtues as the results of reason-disciplining emotions. He describes virtues as lying at a reasonable mean between two extremes, in the case of courage between cowardice (a lack of courage) and foolhardiness (disregard for risks).

In order to judge what action the virtue requires, you need first to know what end is being served, connecting the consequentialist approach with virtue. Courage requires that we take an appropriate amount of risk relative to the importance of our goals. A cost that we might reasonably pay in order to achieve something important will be irrational to pay for something trivial, so the rational side of us must harness our emotions with a judgement about how much a goal is worth.

Obviously the individual still needs strength and integrity, but these too can be developed, provided that the environment is supportive. In the professional setting this demands a general consensus about goals and principles, training, and supportive leadership involving professional development, team building and supervision. At this level the standards of good line management are essential skills for fostering ethical practice.

Ethical skills

Critical reasoning is the skill of being able to analyse situations and reason out the best decision to take. In this chapter we conclude the development of skills in critical reasoning. The previous two chapters introduced the mechanics of constructing a valid and sound argument to justify a view or belief. In this chapter we examine a couple of traps into which it is easy to fall. These traps in reasoning are called *fallacies*. A common fallacy is the 'naturalistic fallacy' where you assume that because something is natural, or perhaps traditional or 'normal', it must be good (such as giving information to the police, as Cara did). Of course natural things may be good, but they aren't necessarily good. A typical example is the appeal to the role that the natural order of things plays in debates over sexual morality. Another fallacy is the slippery slope argument where it is assumed that a small transgression must lead to a worse one. One example is the argument that 'soft' drugs always lead people into addiction to hard drugs. Other common fallacies include:

- the normative mistake of thinking that things we think *should* be true really are;
- fallacies of equivocation where we slide between two different senses of one word, such as in the famous headline 'police begin campaign to run down jaywalkers';
- *ad hominem* appeals to authority where we either discount a claim because of an irrelevant feature of the person making it or believe a claim because of the position of the person making it as Cara did; and
- the fallacy of composition where we illicitly generalise a conclusion from a few examples to a whole class, such as trying to justify a racist assumption based on experience with a couple of individuals.

What fallacies have in common is a problem of justification or warrant. After all, some examples do allow us to draw inductive conclusions; some people are authorities and are entitled to be believed, sometimes small wrongs do lead people into worse wrongdoing. A fallacy is a mistake simply because a surface plausibility can lead us to make conclusions for which have don't have appropriate evidence. The challenge posed by fallacies is to recognise when we are using flawed reasoning by always asking why we believe the conclusion in the particular case. The process of argument or debate from which groups of people derive shared beliefs or values is the single best way to expose fallacies, because what will seem obvious to one person will provoke a question or objection from someone else, protecting each of us from falling into the trap. Over time practice in critical reasoning makes it easier to spot fallacies, but as a rule the more you expose your beliefs to criticism by others the more likely you are to see the problems in your own reasoning.

There are many lists of formal and informal fallacies in textbooks and on the internet. It would be a good idea to study these lists and conduct the exercise of coming up with a few real-world examples to sharpen your awareness of how often these flaws in reasoning crop up.

Ethical knowledge

The major piece of theoretical knowledge to add to your vocabulary is the concept of a dilemma as introduced in talking about Cara's case. The word dilemma is often used in modern English to refer to any moral problem, but properly speaking a dilemma is a conflict. In logic a dilemma is simply a point where an argument splits, where we say 'either this or that'. In moral theory a dilemma is a decision–problem where we have reasons that support taking more than one action where time or resources won't allow both. Instead of reasons in favour of two choices, we can easily have problems where we must do something, but none of the options available are without moral costs.

In Cara's case the challenge is to meet two apparent obligations, a social obligation to respect the law and assist the authorities, in conflict with a professional obligation to protect her client's privacy. In this case the two duties are in direct conflict; doing one thing means not doing the other. In different dilemmas the conflict may be indirect, simply a result of a lack of time or resources. An example of the negative sort of dilemma is when a shortage of resources means that someone must be denied access to a service and workers must decide whom to dedicate more time to, as in the case study in chapter 2.

Sarah Banks and Robin Williams (2005) employ a very useful distinction between dilemmas, problems and issues. Only dilemmas involve the likelihood that we will have to sacrifice some moral obligation. Problems are in principle resolvable. Issues need a lot of work to clarify, involving perhaps a lot of doubt about the facts, the values at stake or the ultimate balance of reasons at work. It is important to be clear if you are facing a dilemma, a problem or an issue, because to mislabel the moral challenge may easily divert you away from possible solutions. In particular, if a problem is set up as having only two clearly understood outcomes, it is easy to miss alternatives and compromises.

A major way to resolve a conflict of any sort is to look again at your goals and the values that define those goals. Properly defining the values of the profession will allow you to decide just which values have the greatest importance, on balance, in any situation you face, and so will permit you to make hard decisions without being debilitated by doubt. Just because there isn't always a way to reconcile competing imperatives doesn't mean that it isn't possible to make a decision. Refusing to make a decision is a kind of action, and you will be just as responsible for the consequences of that decision as for any other.

Conclusion

All of the modes of ethical reasoning combined with the teleological method can help to better understand Cara's problem that opened this chapter. Accepting that she faces a real dilemma, the conflict between two obligations cannot be easily explained away. Nevertheless it ought to be possible to resolve the conflict in favour of a particular claim about what, all things considered, she ought to have done. This will also reveal a great deal about what her manager should have done.

As we discuss in chapter 7 the rules governing confidentiality are not absolute. They are expressions of the value of respect for persons and the principle of autonomy that arises from this value. This value must lead us to respect all persons, so when the rule of client confidentiality based on this value conflicts with consequences for other people the rule can give way (when the consequences are bad enough). Once the proper balance is generally understood and widely endorsed all that remains is for Cara to stick to her position under pressure, an expression of the virtue of courage.

Putting these things into practice involves the set of practices, rules, attitudes and skills that are often summed up as 'professionalism'. To our definition of professionalism from chapter 2, we now add that professionalism makes a normative demand that social workers (with their defined and socially important telos, and a set of special skills and obligations) should consistently rise to meet the challenges of their work.

When we say that professionalism is a normative concept, we mean that we can hold people to account for their professionalism. We could criticise Cara for a lack of good judgement or competence because she was not sure of her position, or was unwilling to assert herself in the face of pressure from the police. We might also criticise her boss for not having trained her staff well enough, for not offering sufficient support during a crisis, or for being judgemental and punitive. All these failures add up to a lack of leadership.

Now that Part One is concluded, we have laid the foundation for ethical social work practice as part of considering the challenges social work faces in our postmodern environment. The virtue of open-mindedness, skills in informal logic and knowledge of teleology introduced in chapter 1 can be summarised as practical reasoning. Taken together with situational awareness and the technique known as satisficing we get moral courage, the ability to make hard decisions. The virtue of moral courage combined with an ability to avoid pitfalls in moral reasoning and knowledge of the kinds of ethical challenges we face produces the capacity for critical reflection. This ability to think carefully and then to act is the basis of the practical discipline of ethics.

In the following chapters we will look more closely at how this ethical capacity is employed. We will examine the telos of social work, the role of codes and rules, and how principles of social work ethics apply in the client-work-agency arena (Payne 2005), for example the role of professional autonomy, a capacity that was clearly not being displayed in Cara's case.

Study tasks

1   Reread the case study at the beginning of this chapter. Consider Cara's difficult position and then attempt to answer the following questions. Don't worry that you may find this hard, just write what you think. What should Cara have done?

- If you disagree with her choices, what do you think she lacked that would have helped her make the right choice?
- What should Cara's supervisor have done?
- What sorts of practices, before and after the event, could the supervisor impose to avoid things going as badly as they did?
- Why do you think the police acted as they did?
- What could the police have done to make things better?
- How might the process of justification have helped avoid these problems?
- Under what circumstances do you think people lose their right to confidentiality of their personal details?
- What does your code of ethics have to say about confidentiality and when it might be overridden?

2   From the information you have about Cara's situation, write down possible solutions from each of these perspectives:

- Consequentialist
- Deontological

Are the two solutions different? If so, in what ways? How do these solutions compare with the one you devised above?

3   In Cara's position, what virtues would be most important?

Further reading

Banks, S. and Williams, R. 2005, 'Accounting for Ethical Difficulties in Social Welfare Work: Issues, problems and dilemmas', *British Journal of Social Work*, vol. 35, no. 7, pp. 1005–22.

Bellamy, R. 1992, *Liberalism and Modern Society*, Polity, Cambridge. Bellamy explores the development of liberalism with regard to Britain and some European states and discusses the work of the likes of Mill, Durkheim and Weber.

Hollis, M. and Howe, D. 1987, 'Moral Risks in Social Work', *Journal of Applied Philosophy*, vol. 4, pp. 123–33. A useful discussion of the idea of moral risk and its application to social work practice. It is especially helpful in showing how we can accept the reality of moral risk without using this as an excuse for defensive practice or denying responsibility in hard cases.

Mill, J.S. 1987, *On Liberty*, ed. Gertrude Himmelfarb, Penguin, Harmondsworth. There are many other editions of this easy-to-read and very short work. It is the foundation of modern liberalism, of interest both as a classic and because it shows how a utilitarian thinker can derive a framework of human and civil rights from a combination of consequentialist and deontological concerns. As such it is a good source for the kind of pluralistic method of ethics we use in this book.

Rachels, J. 2003, *The Elements of Moral Philosophy* (4th edn), McGraw-Hill, New York. This is an excellent introduction to the various approaches to moral philosophy and the ethical analyses built upon them. It can be used as a workbook, going systematically through every chapter, or as a resource.

Websites

Internet Encyclopedia of Philosophy, <http://www.iep.utm.edu/>. This excellent resource is a vast and growing collection of cross-referenced articles written by leading philosophers and ethicists around the world. For this chapter try:

- <http://www.iep.utm.edu/b/bentham.htm>. The entry on Jeremy Bentham is of interest largely because the exposition of Bentham's thought shows how a liberal political philosophy could grow out of a utilitarian or consequentialist ethics. It illustrates nicely why we should not fall into the trap of thinking that apparently quite distinct schools of thought do not influence or support each other.
- <http://www.iep.utm.edu/m/milljs.htm>. The entry on J.S. Mill shows how the transition from utilitarian social policy to liberal politics was made.

Stanford Encyclopedia of Philosophy <http://plato.stanford.edu/>. This is worth using as a starting point for further explorations of ethical theory.

We will be using articles from these two sites throughout the book. For example:

- Rosalind Hursthouse's article on virtue theory at the Stanford Encyclopedia <http://setis.library.usyd.edu.au/stanford/entries/ethics-virtue/>. Hursthouse is one of the leading modern exponents of virtue theory. Obviously she tends to argue in favour of virtue ethics as a complete theory, as opposed to part of a pluralistic ethics, but it is nevertheless a very complete introduction to the approach.
- Walter Sinnott-Armstrong's introduction to consequentialism in the Stanford Encyclopedia <http://setis.library.usyd.edu.au/stanford/entries/consequentialism/> is also an excellent overview of this theoretical modality written by a leading exponent.

- Robert Johnson's entry on Kant at the Stanford site
  <http://setis.library.usyd.edu.au/stanford/entries/kant-moral/>
  will usefully complete an overview of the three major modalities.
  The work focuses on Kant, but it also gives a taste of how deontological or duty-based theories work.
- <http://setis.library.usyd.edu.au/stanford/entries/liberalism/>
  provides Gerald Gaus and Shane D. Courtland's thoughts on
  liberalism as both a philosophy and as a political doctrine.

Internet Encyclopedia of Philosophy <http://www.iep.utm.edu/f/
fallacies.htm>. An article on fallacies—a useful place to start exploring
the world of formal reasoning.

Part two
Meeting the challenge—social work ethics

Having looked at the challenges facing social workers in Part One, including the social-political-ideological context in chapter 1, the agency-professional context in chapter 2 and the different approaches to ethics in chapter 3, in Part Two we examine how social work responds to these challenges. In this chapter, we examine the role of ethics in post-modern social work and where codes of ethics fit.

4
Codes of ethics

Bill is a caseworker whose agency has a contract with another agency to provide casework services to a number of group homes. Each group home cares for up to seven children and is run by a married couple. The wife is employed full time by the agency as a house mother, while the husband is expected to go out to work, receiving only a small remuneration for undertaking day-to-day maintenance such as cutting the lawn.

During a visit to one of the group homes to meet with 16-year-old Matthew in preparation for his moving to an independent living situation, Matthew disclosed that the house-father had assaulted him. Further discussion suggested that this was not an isolated instance, it having occurred on a number of occasions over the last six months since the house-father had been made redundant from his job.

Bill's ethical dilemma was that he felt he should refer the incident to the group home manager in the first instance. He believed that it was the group home agency's responsibility to investigate and determine the most appropriate course of action. If nothing else he tended to feel that his first duty was to notify the group home manager. However, he was not confident that the matter would be properly investigated and he was concerned about repercussions for Matthew. He also thought that if the other children in the group home under sixteen years of age were at risk of harm, he had a statutory obligation to notify them to the child welfare department.

Given his concerns, Bill decided to notify his manager in the first instance. His manager confirmed Bill's views that the other children might be at risk of harm and they should be notified to the department. Bill's manager also advised him to refer Matthew's assault to the police as, being over fifteen, Matthew could not be notified. They agreed that Bill should contact the group home manager and set up a meeting to discuss their concerns.

Things then seemed to happen very quickly. Before Bill could get around to notifying the group home manager of what had been decided he received an irate and abusive phone call from the group home manager. Bill was accused of being disloyal, in breach of the confidentiality agreement between the two agencies, in respect of which legal action was threatened and that he was no longer welcome at any of the agency's group homes. At this point Bill's manager intervened and contacted the group home manager for a meeting.

This case study is based on a real-life scenario experienced by one of the authors. Working for two bosses can create real problems, particularly when different values are being employed to inform decision-making. Bill is feeling torn between conflicting loyalties and duties but he appears to have no basis from which to make a decision. In such situations a code of ethics is invaluable for providing guidance as to the best course of action to pursue. Even if directed to act in a way that contradicts your principles and values, most codes of ethics recognise an employer's right to give directions that employees have to follow, so long as they are not illegal.

The successful use of a code involves more than it being a document you can turn to when an ethical crisis develops. To successfully use your code you need to internalise it and reconcile your values with those of the code. In doing so you not only become aware of your own values, but you are also in a stronger position to make ethically justifiable decisions rather than wondering what you should do. Finally, you can contribute to the improvement of the code itself, by debating it with your colleagues and others with whom you work. As a postscript we note that agreements cannot override legislated reporting requirements.

Social work codes of ethics in a postmodern context

Traditionally, codes of ethics have been the key tool for spelling out what values a profession has. In order to do this they also usually explain the profession's purpose and functions, its ethical values and principles, and sometimes specify standards of professional practice.

In the postmodern context, the role of codes of ethics has become highly controversial. In addition, the relevancy of codes of ethics is under challenge through the use of workplace and licensing codes of conduct. Just as various factors in our globalised world pose challenges and opportunities for social work, so too do they bring into question the role of codes of ethics for all the professions. In chapter 1 we mentioned Bauman's example of how codes can be used to avoid ethical practice, rather than to enhance it—gone are many of the old certainties, and the old structures. Now we will consider what role social work codes of ethics might play in the postmodern environment—whether they are irrelevant or dangerous, as claimed by some authors—and what they can contribute to a profession fuelled by a focus on ethical practice.

Purpose and function of codes of ethics

Codes of ethics are documents that aim to identify the broad values, principles and standards of ethical conduct on which a particular profession is based. For example, both the National Association of Social Workers (NASW) and the Australian Association of Social Workers (AASW) state that their codes have a number of purposes. Although differently worded, in essence the purposes are similar. They include to:

• identify core values and principles that underpin social work;
• provide a guide and standard for ethical social work conduct to which the general public can hold social workers accountable;
• help social workers in ethical reflection and decision-making; and
• act as a basis for investigating and judging whether a social worker has been unethical through a formal complaints process.

These days, codes of ethics, at least in social work, usually contain a statement about the purpose or definition of the profession as well. For example, the recent *Ethics in Social Work, Statement of Principles* by the International Federation of Social Workers (IFSW 2004) begins with the IFSW's definition of social work, moves onto a statement of general ethical principles in two broad categories and concludes with a list of twelve general guidelines on professional conduct that are expected to be elaborated/modified by individual member countries according to local context. Most of the national social work codes of ethics we have studied contain all these elements, though in a variety of structures.

Banks (1998) identifies four general functions of codes of ethics, namely that codes:

• are a guide to conduct and ethical decision-making;
• protect users from malpractice or abuse;
• contribute to the 'professional status' of social work; and
• establish and maintain professional identity.

Banks points out that codes guide practice and protect service users *not* by prescribing specific actions and detailed do's and don'ts, but rather by acting as a sort of 'professional pledge' on the part of the worker to be a certain sort of person—trustworthy, honest, skilled and respectful. Indeed, the Indian social work code is written as a personal pledge. Each value begins 'I pledge to' and social workers must sign it as a personal undertaking (Pawar 1999). The implied promise in all codes to be a certain sort of person emphasises the importance of 'virtues' in social work ethics, and reminds us how the personal and the professional are intertwined.

Banks also discusses how codes can maintain and establish professional identity. This point is particularly important in a profession like social work where there is such a variety of types of work and work settings. If the code provides a clear expression of our professional values, adherence to it may be the only thing we all have in common. Banks stresses that to fulfil this purpose, the code must be updated, discussed and debated within the social work community.

Having broadly described what codes are supposed to do, and given the complex postmodern environment in which we live, there are three possibilities for the role of codes of ethics in social work today: whether they are dangerous, whether they are irrelevant, and whether they can be tools for unifying and empowering a profession.

Are social work codes dangerous?

There is considerable evidence that social work codes, or rather misuse of them, can be dangerous, and inadvertently may be the cause of unethical actions. Here is a true case study from Western Australia.

In 1991 a four-year-old girl was referred by a hospital social work department to a non-government agency for emergency foster care while her mother received in-patient treatment. In turn, the child was referred by a worker in this agency to an approved foster home that had been used frequently for short- and long-term care of children. In this home was a 15-year-old youth who was a ward of the state and who had a previous record of sex offences against young children. Also in the home were the four-year-old grandchild of the foster parents and another young foster child. The sex offending history of the youth was avowedly unknown to these foster parents and to the social worker who had approved the foster home for the youth some months previously. On the other hand, this information was very well known to the youth's long-term foster parents, from whose care he had finally been removed in 1990. Four days after her arrival in the home, the four-year-old girl died as a result of being raped by the youth (Harries 1996).

This case, like the famous North American Tarasoff case, illustrates how poor practice, presumably supported by misguided ideas of prioritising confidentiality over client safety and welfare, can eventuate in tragic and unintended consequences. When ethical standards and principles are applied out of context, either to clients or colleagues, serious harm can result. Across the western world over the past few years, the media has been full of stories about child sexual assault by workers in institutions under various auspices. Presumably many of their colleagues knew about, or suspected, such abuse but it was easier to maintain confidentiality than to do something about the issue. Clearly it is possible that the standards expressed in codes of ethics, if applied in isolation from the other values and principles also in the code, can result in tragic consequences.

Another lesson from this type of situation is the damaging consequences that can occur when people do not understand the differences between practice standards and higher order principles. It has been a very common trap for newly graduated social workers to promise blanket confidentiality (a practice standard coming from a higher order principle of respect for persons) and then discover that they cannot keep their promise or, that if they do, real harm might eventuate. By not understanding the differences between practice standards and higher order principles, or by mixing them up and giving more priority, say, to confidentiality than to the principle from which it came, social workers can get into a great deal of trouble (we discuss this in more detail in chapter 7). This underlines the importance of making ethics a priority in social work education. If ethics is to drive our profession, however, social workers need to become ethically articulate.

A final way that it has been argued that codes of ethics are dangerous is if they are used more as self-serving weapons of a profession or organisation than as tools to defend the public and promote ethical practice. De Maria (1997) argues that codes protect employing organisations rather than whistleblowers or social workers who are trying to defend their clients' rights. At the heart of these kinds of arguments is again the issue of codes having different principles that can be used in isolation from each other. A social worker criticising an organisation for cutting or denying services to a client on the grounds of social justice, for example, may be disciplined for breaching the organisation's confidentiality. A related danger is that a worker could argue that they don't have to worry about social justice because it is not related to their type of work, though they believe that others in the profession will be taking care of it. When people pick and choose which aspects of a code they will follow in this way, Kultgen (1988) argues, codes become a cynical exercise in window dressing.

Our response to these kinds of criticisms is that, yes, codes can be vulnerable to such abuses. What is needed is a strong, collective view on the use of codes, coming from the profession as a whole. With a public, visible commitment to ethical practice by a strong professional association and active ethical debate among practitioners, we can ensure that codes are not misused in such ways.

Are codes of ethics irrelevant?

In chapter 1 we discussed how theorists using postmodern perspectives question whether there is a single 'truth'. Instead, many postmodern writers argue that there are multiple realities, or discourses that colour how people see the world, rather than a single 'truth'. This line of thinking leads to the conclusion that codes of ethics are irrelevant to modern life, because they do not reflect the multiple realities that exist within the same society (Gray, M. 1995; Wood 1997; Banks 1998; Noble and Briskman 1998). For example, indigenous groups in Australia and New Zealand have criticised social work codes of ethics because they ignore indigenous perspectives and understandings.

In the eyes of some theorists, professional codes of ethics enforce the dominant, oppressive voices of the most powerful, leaving out alternative and diverse cultural perspectives. Both Pawar (1999) and Noble and Briskman (1998) have highlighted the individualistic assumptions underlying the Australian social work code of ethics, which excludes notions of collective responsibility as found in indigenous communities. In later work, Briskman and Noble (1999) discuss the possibility of devising more inclusive codes, citing the revised New Zealand social work code as an example.

Another reason codes of ethics are argued to be irrelevant is that social workers simply do not use them. Research into ethical practice in North America (Holland and Kilpatrick 1991) reveals that social workers do not refer to their codes at all when facing ethical dilemmas. A study of seven years of complaints (Bush 1996) also offers support to the argument that we don't use our code to bring social workers to account. Over the seven years (1986–93) there were 27 queries about complaints, ending up in only thirteen formal complaints. Of these thirteen, for various reasons only five proceeded to the hearing and investigation process. Of these five, only one social worker was excluded from membership of the professional association. On the other hand, during the same time, there were 49 consultations about how to act ethically. While we could hope that only one social worker in the state behaved so unethically as to deserve exclusion during these seven years, this seems to be very optimistic. It is more likely that neither professionals nor the public knew how to use the social work code of ethics to deal with social workers who behaved unethically. This lack of awareness in itself could render codes of ethics irrelevant.

One of the greatest challenges to codes of ethics comes from workplace and licensing codes of conduct to guide and inform employees and practitioners. One of the reasons professional codes of ethics are being seen as irrelevant is to do with the combination of low membership of social work associations and the increasing use being made of organisational codes of conduct. These codes tend to be more specific than professional codes of ethics, and in some situations spell out exactly what an employee should do. We argue that in today's workplace, in which work practices are shaped by neo-liberal values, codes of ethics provide social workers with a reference point from which to not only evaluate the impact and ethical worth of policies and procedures, but also the codes of conduct of employers. As set out earlier, codes of ethics reflect the values, principles and standards of ethical conduct of a profession and they apply to all members of the professional association in each country. In comparison, workplace codes of conduct tend to relate to standards of service, are based on values of the employing organisation and their principles and practice standards, apply to every employee rather than particular professions and are limited to the employing organisation. Similar comments can also be made regarding the codes of licensing authorities.

Writers, such as De Maria (1997), contend that codes of ethics are irrelevant to social work because they cannot realise the promise of providing clear direction to social workers due to internal inconsistencies. Critics, such as Kultgen (1988), and Collingridge's (1995) and Hugman's earlier works (Hugman and Smith 1995), take these arguments further and claim that it is the pluralistic basis of codes that causes the internal contradictions in the first place. These and other authors have argued that there is an irreconcilable conflict between the ethical modes we discussed in chapter 3. On the one hand, it is claimed the duty-based or Kantian approach leads to an emphasis on individual rights and responsibilities, while on the other the utilitarian approach (the most common version of consequentialism) focuses more on collective outcomes and this leads to irreconcilable differences (Hugman 1996, cited in Noble and Briskman 1998).

Consider recent debates about torture. To a person committed to a duty-based or deontological approach, torture is a fundamental violation of individual human rights and cannot be justified under any circumstance. To those subscribing to a consequentialist or utilitarian approach, the collective good that may be achieved by gaining information about possible terrorist attacks may justify torture in some instances. People coming from within pure forms of either of these ethical modes could easily reach opposing conclusions about what the ethically right action is when confronted with a person who is believed to be withholding such knowledge. A code of ethics that includes both modes and assumes they are absolutes cannot give proper guidance to interrogators of a person suspected of withholding this information.

Similarly Collingridge argues that the very plurality of codes (including opposing principles) 'allows them to evade collective responsibility for clearly defining and articulating what they stand for, except in some vague and generalised way' (1995: 70). At the irrelevant end of the possible consequences spectrum, this means that codes become so general that they are meaningless and cannot be used to solve specific problems—an issue also commented on by social work practitioners in Noble and Briskman's (1998) study of how social workers use their codes.

Can codes of ethics empower social work?

It is interesting to note that both Hugman (2003, 2005) and Collingridge (an author of this book) have changed their opinions about whether the pluralistic nature of codes, including the supposedly contradictory values and principles, is a problem. Rather than being a weakness, we would argue that it is a strength of a code to include different moral principles. It is not the function of codes to tell professionals what to do in specific circumstances. Instead, codes are there to provide a structure for the various values, principles and standards that need to be taken into account when the practitioner is making a decision. It is the person's responsibility to decide how to act ethically—not a code of ethics'. We have seen how codes and regulations that are too specific can lead to evasion of responsibility rather than to ethical practice. As argued in chapter 3 the heart of exercising professional judgement is to try to balance different ethical values and principles in a pluralistic exercise.

Sometimes the person may decide one principle is more important than another, sometimes they may try to maximise several. This is why professionals, not rule-bound automatons, are needed in social work.

While it is possible that codes of ethics can be irrelevant or even dangerous, depending on their interpretation and how (or whether) social workers and the public use them, it is also possible that social work codes of ethics can empower social workers and offer them a firm foundation from which to take an ethical stand in practice. Perhaps you have known a social worker who was able to empower their clients and 'make a difference', and this inspired you to become involved in this profession. In the midst of stories of the ineffectiveness of social work in the face of the forces of postmodernism, and of the irrelevance or misuse of codes of ethics, there are also stories of social workers 'making a difference' and of how codes can be used to empower practitioners to stand up to those with whom they disagree. For example, recently we were told of an experienced social worker who used his professional ethical principles to argue successfully to be able to undertake long-term intervention in a particular case, despite his agency's policy that clients could only be seen for short-term assessment. A recent example from the United States is of a social worker appointed for an eight-month term as the chair of the Special Commission to Study Sexual Orientation Discrimination in Maryland in 2000/01. Faced with a new arena for practice, Geoffrey Greif called on his code of ethics for guidance and concluded:

What I take away from the experience is a profound respect for our Code of Ethics, the breadth of our literature, and my training. Almost everywhere I looked in the Code, I found relevance to my new role. Whether in social work's commitment to service, social justice, or the enhancement of human well-being, the support is there for the social worker as social change agent (Greif 2004: 280).

If social work values and the codes of ethics that define them are to realise their potential of becoming tools of empowerment, or a way of unifying an increasingly diversifying profession as in Banks's (1998) vision, we will have to make some significant changes. If, contrary to the current evidence, social workers as a whole were well aware of their codes of ethics, used them as living documents and as tools for arguing their clients' cases, and participated in debating them so that they become ever stronger, social work itself would be in a much better position to realise its purposes. We need to bring in ethics from the margins of social work education and practice, and place it at the forefront of professional consciousness.

With a strong code of ethics to which all social workers are committed and involved in creating, social workers will be able to lobby much more effectively for the interests of their clients. A well-known and empowering code would also protect the public and, specifically, social work clients more effectively from malpractice because basic standards would be better understood. Writers such as Banks (1998) and Hugman (2003) speculate that such a code would promote more egalitarian and inclusive relationships between client groups and social workers, and could fundamentally alter the nature of the relationship into a more respectful collegiality and alliances that acknowledge difference without assuming superiority.

For the code of ethics to empower you as a social worker, there are some key questions you should ask (see Study tasks at the end of this chapter). Consider them in light of your own code. If you cannot answer 'yes' to questions 2–10, think about how you might modify your code. Then you will be beginning to operate in the arena of ethical practice where ethics becomes the life force of your professional identity, because you will be actively thinking about your code and how it applies in practice.

Recent developments in social work codes of ethics

Banks (2001) points out that every country with a social work profession has developed some codification of the values, principles and standards on which social work practice is based, although these codes have different emphases, depending on local situations. By examining a number of countries' codes of ethics, we can see how social work deals with the three ethical modes outlined in chapter 3: virtue-based ethics (or the ethical character of the social worker), deontological approaches (from which springs the notion of rights and duties) and consequentialist approaches (from which derive notions of social justice).

Social work, it seems, is responding to the challenges of the post-modern era and some of the critiques outlined in Part One, if recent changes to several countries' social work codes of ethics are any indication. For example, from her survey of many countries' codes of ethics, Banks wrote in 1995 that Australia was the only country to explicitly incorporate social justice as a 'core value' in its code of ethics, on an equal par with the wellbeing of individuals. The AASW maintained this focus on social justice during the major revision to the code in the late 1990s (AASW 2000). Today both the North American (NASW 1999) and the British (BASW 2002) codes similarly emphasise both of these principles. The homepage of the Canadian Association of Social Workers states, 'CASW promotes social justice and well-being for all Canadian residents' (CASW 2005). It seems that some convergence is occurring, at least in the western world, perhaps as a response to the forces of globalisation and postmodernism.

In July 2000, the IFSW adopted a new definition of social work at its general meeting in Montreal, Canada. This new international definition of social work also stresses principles of human rights and social justice. We introduced it in chapter 1 and repeat it here:

> The social work profession promotes social change, problem solving in human relationships and the empowerment and liberation of people to enhance well-being. Utilising theories of human behaviour and social systems, social work intervenes at the points where people interact with their environments. Principles of human rights and social justice are fundamental to social work (IFSW 2002).

Following suit in April 2002, the BASW revised its code of ethics and embraced the new IFSW definition, along with much of the spirit, structure and content of the Australian code. Meanwhile the IFSW was revising its own code, and in July 2002 released a draft document titled *Ethics in Social Work, Statement of Principles*. This document, with modifications following worldwide consultations, was adopted in October 2004 at the international meeting of the IFSW held in Adelaide, and has replaced the 1994 'The Ethical Principles and Standards of Social Work' document.

IFSW: *Ethics in Social Work, Statement of Principles* (2004)

The IFSW document is elegant in its simple wording and brevity. It forms a useful baseline for considering social work codes in general. Less than four pages long, it is divided into five sections. The 'background' sets out the purpose of IFSW's work on ethics ('to promote ethical debate and reflection in the member organisations and among the providers of social work in member countries as well as in schools of social work and among social work students'), noting that 'By staying at the level of general principles, the IFSW statement aims to encourage social workers across the world to reflect on the challenges and dilemmas that face them and make ethically informed decisions about how to act in each particular case.' The preface clarifies that some ethical challenges and problems facing social workers are specific to particular countries, others are common. Four problem areas for social workers are described:

- the fact that social workers' loyalty is often in the middle of conflicting interests;
- the fact that social workers function as both helpers and controllers;
- the conflicts between the duty of social workers to protect the interests of the people they work with and demands for efficiency and utility; and
- the fact that resources in society are limited.

The definition of social work is followed by a list of seven international human rights declarations and conventions which, it is claimed, form common standards of achievement and recognise rights that are accepted by the global community.

The fourth section of the IFSW document lists the two major principles on which social work rests:

- the principle of 'Human Rights and Human Dignity'; and
- the principle of 'Social Justice'.

It is noted that these principles are to apply to all persons, and to society as a whole as well as the people with whom social workers work.

Four elements of human rights and human dignity are identified:

- respecting the right to self-determination;
- promoting the right to participation;
- treating each person as a whole; and
- identifying and developing strengths.

Five elements of social justice are outlined:

- challenging negative discrimination;
- recognising diversity;
- distributing resources equitably;
- challenging unjust policies and practices; and
- working in solidarity with those who are excluded from society, subjugated or stigmatised, towards an inclusive society.

In its fifth and final section, the IFSW document discusses professional conduct, emphasising that all national associations that are members of the IFSW are responsible for updating their own ethical codes or guidelines, consistent with the IFSW statement. Twelve general guidelines for professional conduct are then laid down. These require social workers to:

- develop and maintain the required skills and competence to do the job;
- not allow their skills to be used for inhumane purposes such as torture or terrorism;
- act with integrity (including not abusing their trusted positions for personal benefit or gain and recognising boundaries between personal and professional life);
- act with compassion, empathy and care in relation to people using their services;
- not subordinate the needs or interests of service users to their own needs or interests;
- care for themselves personally and professionally in the workplace so that they can provide appropriate services;
- maintain confidentiality of service users except when there is a greater ethical requirement;
- acknowledge their sometimes conflicting accountabilities to the people they work with, colleagues, employers, professional association and to the law;
- collaborate with schools of social work to support good quality practical training for social work students;
- foster and engage in ethical debate with colleagues and employers and take responsibility for making ethically informed decisions;
- be prepared to state the reasons for their decisions based on ethical considerations and be accountable for their decisions and actions; and
- work to create conditions in employing agencies and in their countries where the principles of this statement and those of their own national code (if applicable) are discussed, evaluated and upheld.

Are there core values and principles in national codes of ethics?

In a brief survey of social work codes of ethics available through the IFSW website and other means, it appears that across the world social work codes of ethics have many aspects in common, and some important differences. We have already discussed how the dual emphasis on the two principles of individual wellbeing and social justice appears to be becoming shared in western social work codes. It is useful to compare various codes to the latest statement from the IFSW to see how universal the principles, values and guidelines for professional conduct are (while noting Banks's (2001) point that differences in the codes may be due to how long it has been since they were updated, rather than reflecting differences in actual social work practice).

Three of the western English-speaking countries appear to have very similar codes of ethics in both structure and content. The British (BASW 2002), North American (NASW 1999) and Australian (AASW 2000) codes all begin with a statement of values and principles, followed by more detailed prescriptions for professional conduct, variously termed 'Ethical Standards' (NASW) or 'Ethical practice' (AASW and BASW). The New Zealand code (ANZASW 1993), soon to be the Aotearoa/New Zealand code, is currently under review. It is different from all other social work codes in that it includes a 'Bicultural Code of Practice'. Some commentators such as Briskman and Noble (1999) and Hugman (2003) view this development as an interesting model for incorporating diversity and 'otherness'. Others such as Banks (2001) question why this could not have been done in one code instead of writing a separate document for work with Maori people. One of Banks's concerns is that this model could encourage a proliferation of different codes for different groups (2001: 98–9).

The Canadian code, which is older than the British, North American and Australian ones, lists seven 'ethical duties and obligations' that provide the basis for the relationship between the social worker and their client. It specifies that the last three statements are to be seen as ethical responsibilities and are different from the first seven ethical duties and obligations. Due to this distinction, they are not listed as core values/principles in Table 4.1. They include: ethical responsibilities to the workplace, ethical responsibilities to the profession and ethical responsibilities for social change. The last clause in this final statement reads: '10.6: A social worker shall promote social justice.' This code reflects the older view inherent in social work codes, which privileged values and principles relating to the relationship between social workers and their clients (usually assumed to be individuals) over values relating to social justice. Included in the ethical responsibilities for social change is a clause on environmental sustainability: 'social worker shall advocate for a clean and healthy environment and shall advocate the development of environmental strategies consistent with social work principles.'

The Turkish statement of ethical principles and responsibilities of social workers lists 13 ethical principles, which form a mix of the values and principles listed in the other codes, with a notable emphasis on human rights and anti-terrorism.

The Indian code, which was in its sixth draft form in 1996, has some interesting differences from the other codes, highlighted by Pawar (1999). Chief among them is the inclusion of the 'inherent worth and dignity of people' principle, where people are seen as 'part of nature, needing to live in harmony with other non-human existence'. Another interesting feature of this declaration is its commitment to 'solidarity and partnership with the marginalised people' and peaceful, non-violent approaches to 'resolving conflicts with self, others and the environment'.

A final feature of the Indian code which we find especially interesting is the second of three values listed in the value framework: the value described as working towards 'the overall well-being of people in the spirit of Sarvodaya [see Table 4.1], through the achievement of the following goals'. Three goals are then listed:

- equity and non-discrimination in relation to a number of issues;
- social, economic, political and legal justice; and
- people-centred development, in the spirit of Swarajya and

democracy ... where people participate to determine their life-styles and goals for development (Social Work Educators' Forum 1997: 337).

The value in these three goals incorporates aspects of social justice and self-determination into the one value. These values in western ethics are seen as distinct and sometimes at odds with each other because they come from different ethical modes—self-determination from deontological or rights-based approaches, and social justice, often seen as coming from consequentialist or outcomes-focused modes (Clark 2000; Hugman 2003).

In his comparison of the Australian and Indian documents, Pawar (1999) notes that despite its emphatic commitment to social justice, the Australian code is still unbalanced in favour of individualised practice with clients. He argues that the use of words such as 'client', 'assistance', 'management' and 'administration' militate against empowerment, participation and people-centred development, as exists in the Indian declaration. Instead 'an iron curtain of unequal parallels' (1999: 83) has been built, or a giver/receiver division into the AASW social justice agenda.

What makes a good social worker—the telos of social work

Despite the differences, in general, when considered against the recent IFSW statement, most of the codes in Table 4.1 contain the major elements of the IFSW document. The differences in the detail of each country's document depend on the context. It seems that it is possible to identify three broad themes of what makes a good social worker. Together, these comprise the telos of social work. Drawing on the IFSW's definitions, these themes are summarised as:

• respect for the inherent dignity and worth of all people and the human rights that follow from this, including respecting self-determination, promoting participation, treating people as a whole and identifying and developing strengths;

Table 4.1: Comparison of values/principles in some countries' codes of ethics

IFSW Ethics in social work statement of principles	Australian code of ethics (2000)	National Association of Social Workers (USA) code 1999	British Association code of ethics (2002)	Canadian Association code of ethics (1996)	Association of social workers in Turkey (undated)	Declaration of ethics for professional social workers (India 1996)
Human rights and human dignity	Human dignity and worth	Service	Human dignity and worth	Maintain best interest of client	Unique value of every human	Inherent worth and dignity of people, needing to live in harmony with other non-human existence
Social justice	Social justice	Social justice	Social justice	Integrity and objectivity	Self-fulfilment	Working towards the overall wellbeing of people in the spirit of 'Sarvodaya'*
	Service to humanity	Dignity and worth of the person	Service to humanity	Competence	Society should function for maximum benefit of members	Solidarity and partnership with the marginalised people
	Integrity	Importance of human relationships	Integrity	Non-exploitation (limit on professional relationship)	Human rights—UN Declaration	Peaceful and non-violent approaches in the spirit of 'Ahimsa'***
	Competence	Integrity	Competence	Confidentiality	Service	
		Competence		Outside interest	Struggle against social inequality	

Limit on private practice	Social change and justice goals
Ethical responsibilities to workplace	Competence
	Confidentiality and privacy
	Informed consent and participation of clients
	Self-determination, minimum compulsion
	Anti-terrorism, torture or brutal means
	Accept the association's principles and responsibilities

* 'Sarvodaya' is an ideology which mainly emphasises 'Swarajya' (self-reliance, self-rule and self-governance) and 'lokniti' (equity and social justice for all) (Pawar 1999). As part of the description of this value in the Declaration, three goals are identified:

- equity, non-hierarchy and non-discrimination of human groups;
- social, economic, political and legal justice, ensuring satisfaction of basic needs, and integrity and security, universal access to essential resources and protective safeguards for the marginalised people; and
- people-centred development from micro to macro levels where people participate to determine their lifestyles and goals for development.

** 'Ahimsa' means non-violence (Pawar 1999).

- responsibility to promote social justice, both in relation to society in general and the people with whom we work, including challenging negative discrimination, acknowledging diversity, distributing resource equitably, challenging unjust policies and practices and working in solidarity with those who are subjugated, excluded, or stigmatised; and
- behaviour that is ethically sound or 'virtuous', including being competent, acting with integrity, being compassionate and empathic, not putting their own needs above the needs of the people who use their services, being accountable, engaging in ethical debate, caring for themselves professionally, etc.

These three themes are closely related to the three ethical modes discussed in chapter 3: deontological, consequentialist and virtue-based. Respect for human dignity and worth comes from the deontological approach to ethical thinking, the approach which judges whether an action is ethically sound by whether it is in accordance with universal moral rules—in this case whether an action treats a person or group of people with respect and as inherently valuable beings. Social justice derives from the consequentialist mode of ethical thinking, which judges an action as being right by its outcomes—in this case whether policies result in fair and equitable treatment of people and distribution of resources. (These themes are also discussed in more detail in chapter 5 and then applied in chapters 6, 7 and 8.) The standards of professional conduct derive from the Aristotelian virtue-based ethical mode, the idea that social workers must demonstrate certain character traits such as integrity, commitment to high standards of competence, compassion etc. (This theme is developed throughout the book.)

Virtues

We are often told how important the virtue of reflection is for social work. This is especially the case when we are juggling the interactions and impact between our professional code of ethics, our social work practice and other codes of conduct with which we are expected to comply such as our employer's, licensing codes, etc. As a way of working, reflection involves both reflective thinking and discussion with colleagues. (Note that reflection is not the same as reflectiveness, however, you may hear the two words being used interchangeably. Reflectiveness is defined by Fook (2002) as a practice approach based on practice wisdom, rather than empiricism, involving the use of intuition that develops with experience.)

Reflection is a component of praxis. In reflecting upon the relationship of theory to practice and practice to theory, and exploring the linkages between the two, you are engaging in reflective thinking (Fook 2002). Thus with the different codes you have to work with, in reviewing them and their relationship to each other and to practice you are engaged in reflection.

This kind of reflection is important as it assists you to understand how your code guides you in the work environment and helps shape the nature of your relationship with your clients and co-workers. Through cultivating your capacity to reflect you further develop your ability to engage in critical analysis and look behind what is said and written and the assumptions made for the informing values and ideologies.

Perhaps if Bill from our case study had taken the time to reflect on his circumstances he might have handled things a little differently. He could have advised the group home manager of the allegations and that he would take it up with his manager (however, he may not have felt comfortable approaching the group home manager on his own).

Ethical skills

If it is necessary to cultivate the virtue of reflection in order to fully appreciate the significance of codes and to become an ethical practitioner, being able to relate your views and thoughts to others requires you to have good communication skills. Being a good communicator enables us to make clear our values, raise issues of concern about codes and discuss how they impact on our practice.

Communication, or more correctly effective communication, can never be taken for granted. Most of us will have heard that communication is affected by how well the sender communicates, the medium of communication used and how the receiver interprets the communication. Yet as simple as effective communication seems, and with communication being central to the social worker's role, a lot of our time is spent resolving miscommunication. The potential for miscommunication is always high. For example, in a casework setting involving a family of five which is being seen collectively and individually by two caseworkers, there are a possible twenty-five paths of communication. A miscommunication on any path can destabilise the whole situation.

If we are to be effective communicators, we need to appreciate and understand the multiple communications possible in any situation. It is only through considering the variables associated with the sender, medium and receiver that we can begin to communicate effectively. If as social workers we want to make our values transparent to others we need to enhance our communication skills. If Bill had decided to brief the group home manager on the allegations he could have taken a moment to make some rough notes to assist in his briefing. When we feel stressed it is easy to make basic mistakes, a problem that in part can be overcome by having some notes to refer to. Notes can be used to make sure everything is covered and the conversation factual and limited to pertinent issues. Doing so can take a lot of the emotion out of such a meeting.

Ethical knowledge

While it may be convenient at times to think in unitary terms, and so avoid having to consider options, the reality of social work practice is that in most circumstances we find ourselves having multiple options. Viewed from another perspective, every decision taken involves considering competing demands for limited resources. This emphasises why it is important to understand the pluralistic nature of life. Even in the workplace where specific courses of action may be prescribed, adapting Foucualt (1972), it is healthy to ask why things are done this way and not some other way.

We have argued that it is a strength, not a weakness, that codes of ethics are based on a pluralist approach. Codes do not prescribe practice or courses of action. Rather they challenge and guide us to respond in the most appropriate manner, having regard to both the person or persons involved and the context, and taking into account a number of considerations including the consequences of what we do, our duties and fundamental principles, and whether our actions exemplify the kind of person we want to be (whether we are being virtuous). Remember this concept of pluralism is quite different from relativism, as we discussed in chapter 3. Our notion of pluralism is an important piece of ethical knowledge to include in your ethical toolkit.

Conclusion

In summary, being able to reflect on why you acted as you did, to explain your actions to others and to take into account a number of ethical perspectives when making an ethical decision are vital attributes if you are going to develop a caring approach to your social work practice.

In this chapter, we have argued that social work, always an essentially ethical profession, needs to reclaim ethics as its heart and driving force, and to clarify its purpose and functions accordingly. As part of this, the role of codes of ethics needs to be properly understood, the dangers acknowledged and a new collective commitment to codes of ethics as living documents made.

We have argued that if social workers develop a code of ethics that is:

- based on vigorous debate;
- in the forefront of professional consciousness; and
- strongly supported by the profession collectively,

then we will have the opportunity, even with our increasing fragmentation and specialisation, to empower social work to realise its
goals.

Study tasks

1 Have a look at your own country's code of ethics. What are the
   key purposes, principles and standards of practice or conduct?
   How do they compare with the IFSW statement of principles?
2 Would you be able to take on this code as the type of 'personal
   pledge' discussed in this chapter?
3 Does your code provide you with a guide to good practice and a
   basis for judging bad practice? Give some examples.
4 Does your code provide a framework for you to make ethical
   decisions?
5 Does the document empower you to act as a professional and
   exercise professional judgement?
6 Would your client groups or members of the general public be
   able to use your code as a basis to complain about a social
   worker? How accessible is the language in your code?
7 Have you heard or seen a social worker refer to their code of
   ethics?
8 What is your experience of how professional codes of ethics and
   codes of conduct are used in human service organisations?
   Do you know of times when workers have experienced conflict
   between them? What happened?
9 Have you encountered situations where a code of ethics might
   have been useful, but was not used? Or where a code of ethics

was misused? Do you have experiences where codes of ethics have been used to empower practitioners to work ethically? Discuss your answers to these questions with your colleagues or study partners.

10 Are there any changes you would like to see made to your code of ethics? List the changes.

Further reading

Banks, S. 2001, *Ethics and Values in Social Work* (2nd edn), Palgrave Macmillan, Basingstoke, Hampshire; esp. chapter 5 'Professional Codes of Ethics'. An excellent introduction to the fundamental ethical principles of social work, including a comparison of 20 different countries' codes of ethics. Excellent case studies and examples for students and practitioners later in the book.

Coady, M. and Bloch, S. (eds) 1996, *Codes of Ethics and the Professions*, Melbourne University Press, Melbourne. Contains many good articles on the purpose, function and role of professional codes of ethics in various professions. Also experiences of people trying to write and use codes.

Greif, G.L. 2004, 'When a Social Worker Becomes a Voluntary Commissioner and Calls on the Code of Ethics', *Social Work*, vol. 49, no. 2, pp. 277–80. A good example of how one social worker in a new position used his code of ethics proactively to guide his practice and help make decisions.

Reamer, F. 2001, *Social Work Values and Ethics*, Columbia, New York. From the United States, explores values, the NASW code of ethics and ethical dilemmas in direct and indirect practice, lots of case studies.

Websites

International Federation of Social Workers <http://www.ifsw.org/>
continually posts new and revised ethics documents which are referred
to in this book. <http://www.ifsw.org/Publications/4.4.1.pub.html> has
a comprehensive collection of national codes from member countries of
the IFSW.

5
The purpose of social work

To facilitate the transfer of the case management of the Williams family to a non-government organisation, Phoebe Smith (who we met at the start of chapter 2) was asked by her manager to organise a case conference and give a presentation and analysis on the social history and background of the family. Phoebe felt she had to come up with a particularly compelling argument if she was to continue working with the family. So, in addition to inviting the representative from the non-government organisation, and in spite of her manager's directive, Phoebe decided to include another plea to retain the case as part of her presentation.

While acknowledging she had yet to work out the dynamics that troubled the children, Phoebe argued that it was obvious that the high level of conflict between Jill and Nigel, combined with Jill's dependency on Nigel, put the children at risk. Further, Jill and Nigel were barely literate so could not fill out forms or be expected to advocate for themselves in the wider system. Their recurrent financial crises made it impractical to refer them to family counselling until basic survival issues had been resolved. Thus, Phoebe argued, a significant contributing factor was the inability of systems, such as the social welfare system, to accommodate persons such as Jill and Nigel. These systems expected social welfare recipients to be literate, organised and have some social skills. Rather than pursuing knock-backs, Jill and Nigel tend to withdraw, in the process becoming more isolated. Because of this she doubted the capacity of the family to ever be autonomous. However, Phoebe felt that with support and guidance the family would be able to exercise a basic level of decision-making and be self-determining.

Phoebe concluded that the family was as much disadvantaged by an uncaring system which she considered inadequate. Referring to the government's social justice strategy, which her department had endorsed, Phoebe sought to argue that with this family the strategy could only be given effect if the department continued to be involved, even though this conflicted with the department's charter. Only the department, she argued, had the capacity and resources to ensure the family members had the same opportunities in life as others and receive ongoing support and assistance.

Her manager overruled her conclusions, stating that this was not the department's role, that it was up to Jill and Nigel to solve their own problems, that the family, in particular the mother, had to take responsibility for their actions and should not expect the department to constantly prop them up. Coming so soon after her earlier clash with her manager Phoebe Smith felt humiliated, especially as this confrontation was held in front of workers from outside the department.

The situation in which Phoebe finds herself, being pressured to 'contract out' or refer the family on rather than to provide a direct service herself, and to see the problem somehow residing inside the family rather than in a failure of society to provide the resources it needs, is typical of the daily challenges social workers face working within a western neo-liberal environment. It is not enough for Phoebe to deliver her professional assessment and for that to be respected and acted upon; in these days of the erosion of professional autonomy Phoebe has to argue her case along with others and is expected to follow the policy directives of her employer.

Phoebe also seems to be quite isolated in her argument with her manager. We do not know if she has discussed her position with other colleagues inside or outside the department nor what the Williams family think about the situation. In chapter 2 we saw how important it is to work collectively if social workers are to influence policy and work to empower disadvantaged people excluded from the decision-making that affects them. The strategies we discussed there as part of satisficing could also be effective in this situation.

While Phoebe refers in general terms to her organisation's social justice strategy, she makes no mention of her own professional principles or code of ethics. In chapter 4 we saw how organisational codes of conduct can be more visible than professional codes and noted how rare it is for social workers to use their professional code in their daily practice. If the social work code of ethics was better known and debated, and if Phoebe had referred to specific ethical principles to which she is committed as a social worker, her argument would have been much stronger. While it is possible that ethical principles are at the heart of Phoebe's argument, she is not clear about this and does not seem to have the ethical vocabulary to argue her case convincingly.

In the previous chapter we began to explore social work's response to the challenges it faces by discussing the role codes of ethics can play. In the process we identified some fundamental principles that appear to underpin social work around the globe: a commitment to human rights and dignity on one hand, and to social justice on the other, along with commitments to practise certain virtues, expressed as guidelines for professional conduct. These are succinctly laid down in the IFSW statement of ethical principles (IFSW 2004). In this chapter we examine these core principles or the telos of social work practice in more detail. As you explore the principles of human rights and dignity and social justice (the knowledge theme for this chapter), you will also be reminded about the virtue of empathy and skill of self-awareness.

Human rights and human dignity

The first principle listed in the IFSW *Ethics in Social Work, Statement of Principles* is 'human rights and human dignity'. The IFSW expresses it thus:

> Social work is based on respect for the inherent worth and dignity of all people, and the rights that follow from this. Social workers should uphold and defend each person's physical, psychological, emotional and spiritual integrity and well-being (IFSW 2004).

In the section of the document immediately before the ethical principles, the IFSW identifies seven international human rights declarations and conventions which it states are especially relevant to social work practice. The first in the list is the United Nations Universal Declaration of Human Rights, proclaimed by the UN General Assembly in 1948 following the atrocities committed during the Second World War. While valuing human dignity and worth has been a fundamental principle of social work since its inception, linking human dignity and worth with the notion of human rights is a relatively new development for social work. Indeed Reichert (2003: 249) argues forcefully that North American social work has for too long avoided integrating human rights into social work education.

How can we distinguish a human right from other kinds of rights? One of the defining features of human rights is that they are held to be universal, that is, that they apply to all people, regardless of their race, circumstances or any other characteristic. Accordingly, we should bear in mind that they apply equally to our society and are not something we only consider in the context of countries whose cultures are not based on western values. Ife (2001) notes that human rights are also usually understood as being indivisible (they come as a package, one cannot pick and choose), inalienable (they cannot be taken away—a controversial point since the law sometimes sanctions the removal of rights for prisoners), and inabrogable (human rights cannot be traded, given up or given away). He outlines five criteria, all of which must be met before a right can be accepted as a human right. Once a claim meets these criteria and is accepted as being a human right, it takes priority over other competing claims if there is a conflict. The five criteria are:

- The claimed right is necessary for a person or group of people to be able to achieve their full humanity, in common with others.
- The claimed right either applies to all of humanity or to people from specific disadvantaged or marginalised groups for whom realisation of that right is essential to achieving their full human potential.
- There is substantial universal consensus on the legitimacy of the claimed right and support for it across cultural and other divides.
- It is possible for the claimed right to be realised by all legitimate claimants. (This excludes rights to things in limited supply such as the right to own large tracts of land etc.)
- The claimed right does not contradict other human rights (Ife 2001: 10–11).

As with most important ideas, human rights is a highly contested term that carries different meanings depending on the context and discourse within which it is used. Many writers refer to three 'generations' of human rights, although even this idea is debated. Ife (2001) identifies first-generation human rights as being civil and political rights that in their present form come from eighteenth-century Enlightenment ideas and liberal political philosophy. They involve fundamental freedoms associated with the value of the individual such as freedom of speech, free assembly, the right to vote, to a fair trial and so on. Thus first-generation rights are often seen as rights which need to be protected and as being somehow natural. They are expressed as negative rights because they are to be protected and guaranteed, rather than being more positively realised. Ife (2001) notes that first-generation human rights are violated on a daily basis around the world. Social workers involved in first-generation human rights work with individuals, in advocacy and related activities.

Second-generation rights are economic, social and cultural rights that involve the rights of individuals and groups to receive various forms of social services in order to realise their full potential as human beings. As Noyoo, writing about social work and human rights in South Africa, puts it: 'What poverty poses for human rights is that people cannot live dignified lives' (Noyoo 2004: 363). Second-generation rights, which have their origins in nineteenth- and twentieth-century social democracy or socialism, are known as positive rights because they imply a much more active role for the state through various forms of social provision. Helping people realise their second-generation rights is the bread and butter of most social workers, according to Ife (2001). For example, social workers working with people on low incomes (in poverty), in residential care or who are homeless, in health care and education systems, are all helping people to realise their second-generation human rights.

Ife (2001: 37–8) further argues that if social work is a human rights profession, concerned with second-generation rights, it is required to become politically active to seek policy change so that adequate social services are provided. This means that the traditional macro-level aspects of social work, including organisational practice, research, systemic advocacy, social action and policy work are vitally important, given the current trends to reduce social service provision.

Third-generation rights exist at a collective level although individuals benefit from having them. These include rights to economic development, environmental rights such as having clean water, the right to live in a harmonious society etc. Ife notes that while these rights have only been recognised as human rights in the twentieth century in the West, in other cultures such as those influenced by the Confucian tradition collective rights have had fundamental importance for centuries and in some instances take priority over individual first- or second-generation rights. Thus, even the terms 'first-generation', 'second-generation' and 'third-generation' reveal a western bias because they reflect the historical emergence and perceived priority of these categories of rights in western liberal thought. Community development is the main expression of third-generation human rights in social work and, Ife argues, is undervalued in western social work just as third-generation rights are undervalued in western neo-liberal society.

Supporting Ife's view and writing from the United Kingdom, Bowring (2002) argues that neither the United Kingdom nor the United States extend their notion of human rights to social and economic rights, rights which he claims underpin notions of social justice. Further, he argues that social justice can never be realised while liberal interpretations of human rights refuse to acknowledge or address collective and group rights.

Pakulski (2004) adds a disturbing note to the critique of human rights when he distinguishes cultural from social (welfare) rights. He argues that in the process of stalling the development of social rights and dismantling social services, claims for cultural rights have gained ascendancy on a global level. For example, indigenous and gay rights activism across the world have shifted from political and welfare demands to demands for cultural rights—rights to dignified representation in the media and other symbolic spheres (for example education and language) and for acceptance of indigenous lifestyles and culture. He writes:

> The rights to equal representation and maintenance of cultural distinctiveness start to displace social-welfare claims. Demands for these cultural rights may be easier to satisfy than the demands for social rights: their costs do not blow up state budgets and do not trigger fiscal panics. The state can remodel itself as a guardian of cultural pluralism and as a 'licensing board' for identities and lifestyles (Pakulski 2004: 128–9).

Claiming that 'Human rights are the children of globalisation' (2004: 129) Pakulski poses contrasting arguments: while on one hand human rights can extend citizenship rights to offer the hope of empowerment to all peoples, on the other hand there are two pressures threatening that human rights will become meaningless abstractions.

The first is that there are no international institutions capable of defending and enforcing human rights. The current arrangements within the United Nations and its conventions rely on the goodwill of its participants. The second pressure is the one also discussed by Ife and Bowring—the different ways human rights are interpreted by rich and poor nations. Pakulski agrees that affluent nations emphasise the first-generation rights of liberties and political rights, while the poor nations stress the 'survival' rights of second- and third-generation human rights. Without worldwide consensus on what constitutes human rights, and the ability to defend and enforce them, human rights will become meaningless. Similarly Ife (2001) warns that while human rights has the potential to be a powerful perspective from which social work can strive to realise its social justice goals, we must understand the contradictions and criticisms associated with it if we want to realise this potential. He asserts that we need to understand human rights as an evolving discourse that is always changing, but still universal because it is about how we construct universal values about what it means to be human.

Having considered some of the debates and issues associated with human rights, let us see how the IFSW interprets human rights and human dignity. As noted in chapter 4, the IFSW sets out four points in explaining what it means by this term. The first point, *respecting the right to self-determination*, is one of the oldest principles in western social work first documented by Felix Biestek in 1961. This aspect of human well-being is clearly an expression of first-generation human rights, being about the freedom to carry out one's decisions and life choices as long as they do not interfere with the choices of others.

The second and third points: *promoting the right to participation* so that people are *'empowered in all aspects of decisions and actions affecting their lives'* and *treating each person as a whole* including their families, communities, societies and the natural environment, imply second- and third-generation human rights. People require their basic physical and social needs to be met (Maslow, cited in Gray 1991) in order for them to exercise their right to participate and this means having basic income, nutrition, housing, health, security and education. By specifying a holistic concept of the individual as embedded within their family, community, cultural and environmental context, the IFSW sets itself apart from the dominant western neo-liberal view of the individual, and a consequent emphasis only on first-generation human rights. Thus this third part of the definition also provides space for second- and third-generation rights to have equal importance for social workers.

The final part of the IFSW definition of human rights and human dignity emphasises empowerment through *identifying and developing strengths*. Importantly, this emphasis applies not just for work with individuals, but also collectives such as groups and communities, again including second- and third-generation rights. According to Healy: 'The growing popularity of the strengths perspective can partly be attributed to its embodiment of social work values, particularly its emphasis on respect, and service user self-determination' (Healy 2005: 151). Originating in the North American mental health field, partly in opposition to approaches that emphasised pathology and deficits within people who use services, the strengths approach to social work practice emphasises optimism, building on strengths and assets, and working in collaborative partnerships with people who use services (Saleebey 2002). Critiques of this approach include that it does not take sufficient account of structural barriers, that it is founded on liberal beliefs, that the notion of 'strengths' is culturally determined, and also that it relies too much on individuals and communities to help themselves. Nonetheless writers such as Healy (2005) acknowledge that the strengths perspective does provide social workers with a useful platform from which to promote respect for client capacities, perspectives and potential.

In summary then, the latest version of the IFSW (2004) *Ethics in Social Work, Statement of Principles* reveals a vision of human dignity integrated with human rights as one of social work's two foundation ethical principles. The notion of human rights is framed within an understanding of people–within–their–contexts, which includes first-, second- and third-generation human rights as the province of social work. We now consider the second ethical principle in the IFSW statement: social justice.

Social justice and social work

Social justice is the newest principle in social work codes, having only recently appeared on an equal footing with respect for human dignity and worth and the virtuous character traits such as integrity. Social justice first appeared in an international code of ethics in 1976 (Valentine 2005) and was first defined by an association in 1999 (NASW 1999; AASW 2000). However, concern for social justice has a long history in social work, even if not called by that name (Morris 2002; Bisman 2004). For example, Patricia McGrath Morris argues that the shift to a concern for social justice in social work can be seen as early as 1910 in the United States, when Jane Addams, social activist and co-founder of Chicago's Hull House Settlement, was elected as president of social work's then mainstream forum. By 1917, Morris asserts, this organisation had changed its name to the National Conference of Social Work (NCSW) and practitioners had begun to call themselves social workers instead of charity workers. Morris quotes the new president, Grace Abbott, who comments in her presidential address about the name change:

> we have since, by changing the name, tried to unload as belonging to the dead past all mistakes we have made in the name of charity; and perhaps we are also trying with this new name to make ourselves believe that we have arrived at the day when social justice and scientific social treatment make charity and correction unnecessary (Abbott 1924: 4, cited in Morris 2002: 366).

However, social justice is also a highly contested term. Despite the recent lip service to it, to the point where some authors warn that it could become meaningless (Ife 2000; Valentine 2005), there is little consensus about what social justice actually means. The only common view seems to be that in social work there is a conceptual muddle about social justice, and that its meaning has been shaped by social and economic conditions so that it has changed over the years (Scanlon and

Longres 2001; Pinkerton and Campbell 2002; Valentine 2005). Valentine describes nine different meanings of the term in the non-social work literature, none of which have been rigorously explored in social work writings. Valentine also shows how many of these expressions of social justice have been reinterpreted to fit within the dominant neo-liberal context, in a way that is quite removed from their original meanings, to do with promoting the common good (for example, Del Vecchio 1952; Calvez and Perrin 1961).

These warnings about the lack of clarity about social justice only underline the urgency for greater understanding of and debate about the term. At the risk of oversimplifying then, concern with social justice is related to various notions of fairness, inclusiveness, anti-oppressive practice, and the distribution of goods and services, so as to facilitate the common good.

We have discussed how social justice has been seen as the collective or social side of social work, focusing on outcomes or consequences of policies for various groups, sometimes in opposition to an emphasis on individual rights and needs. Sometimes it is seen as the main principle underlying macro forms of social work practice, such as community development and policy work, in contrast to the individual rights principle, which is said to underlie the micro or counselling forms of social work (see Morris 2002 for a more detailed discussion). We challenge this division as a false dichotomy, arguing that social justice and respect for human rights and dignity are both important for macro and micro practice—to be effective, social work needs a commitment to both principles at whatever level it is practised. By only focusing on one or other of the two foundation principles, social work will surely wither and die.

It is important to recognise that social justice is context dependent. The challenge is to find ways of defining social justice that are respectful and inclusive of difference, but do not retreat into cultural relativism. We now turn to examine in more detail the five elements of social justice identified by the IFSW (2004).

Challenging negative discrimination is the first element listed and includes the responsibility to challenge discrimination 'on the basis of characteristics such as ability, age, culture, gender or sex, marital status, socio-economic status, political opinions, skin colour or other physical characteristics, sexual orientation, or spiritual beliefs' (IFSW 2004). This element seems to fall within the conception of social justice as freedom from oppression and domination, which is one of the nine expressions of social justice identified by Valentine (2005). This conception implies that social structures and forces cause social problems and deny people the ability to be self-determining and is explored in detail by Iris Young (1990). Valentine argues that this expression of social justice is based on the intrinsic dignity of and respect for each person, and so avoids the problems of other expressions of social justice that rely on notions of desert or need. Indeed, four of the five elements listed in the IFSW definition appear to flow from this vision of social justice as 'freedom from oppression and domination'.

The second element sets out social workers' obligation to 'recognise and respect the ethnic and cultural diversity of the societies in which they practise, taking account of individual, family, group and community differences' (IFSW 2004). This can be seen as compelling social workers to minimise the oppression of those who are discriminated against on the basis of cultural difference. There is also a positive imperative to value difference: for social workers to incorporate the notion of culture (and gender) minority rights into their understanding of social justice. Gary Craig expresses this most succinctly when he writes: 'For minority ethnic groups this means the right to be culturally different within a society which provides the same social, civil and political rights to all; that is, to be equal but different' (2002: 671). This element underscores how important context is when considering aspects of social justice. It can also be interpreted as being part of the principle of respecting human dignity and worth. Thus the close relationship between the two principles of social justice and human dignity and worth are evident.

Both the fourth and fifth elements of the IFSW definition of social justice also fall strongly within the notion of social justice as freedom from oppression. The fourth one, *challenging unjust policies and practices*, calls social workers to bring to the attention of their employers, policy-makers, politicians and the general public those situations where people are living in poverty, or are otherwise oppressed by unfair policies and practices or inadequate resources. This duty potentially empowers social workers to override specific organisational demands to follow unjust policies or to remain silent about officially sanctioned injustice.

The fifth element, *Working in solidarity*, comes with the 'obligation to challenge social conditions that contribute to social exclusion, stigmatisation or subjugation, and to work towards an inclusive society' (IFSW 2004). This implies that social workers need to work in partnership with oppressed groups and social movements towards social change, rather than working for their improvement from a position of superiority, or on their behalf, as in older versions of professionalism. As Thompson comments:

> The challenge social work faces therefore, is to develop forms of professionalism which are consistent with, and welcoming of, user participation and a commitment to equality and social justice, that is, professionalism based on partnership (2002: 717).

The third element of the IFSW definition of social justice appears to have a slightly different basis from the other four. It directs social workers to distribute the resources at their disposal equitably, with the term 'equitably' explained as 'fairly, according to need'. Because the whole document is deliberately left at the general level, presumably definitions of what is 'fair' and how 'need' is to be determined are left up to the individual country or even organisation or social work setting, thus allowing the notion of social justice to be, again, context dependent. There are many notions of what terms such as 'equitable', 'fair' and 'need' mean. Whether 'fairness' is based on the ideas of procedural fairness in social work as first expressed by Rawls (1971), or notions of distributive justice, which is about the redistribution of goods and services (Taylor 1986; Barry 1989) or some other notion entirely, is deliberately left unspecified. However, what is definite is having an identifiable process to determine fairness and need.

Together, these five elements form a multi-dimensional approach to social justice that can be context-dependent and interpreted to fit different countries' situations. There is a strong challenge to social workers around the world to take on social justice as a core value—both in their work and more generally in relation to society as a whole—and to become actively involved in social justice issues in our globalised world.

Globalisation from below

One way of summing up social work's new commitment to social justice and human rights as part of human dignity is the project of 'globalisation from below'. Writers such as Ife (2000), Brecher, Costello and Smith (2002) and Khinduka (2004) argue that so far, globalisation has been 'top-heavy', with international institutions such as the World Bank and the International Monetary Fund being dominated by the interests of the developed world and, within this, the most powerful groups such as multinational corporations. However, we have also seen that globalisation is a complex process, leading to complex inequalities as well as unexpected opportunities (Pakulski 2004). With the new access to the internet and international communication, previously silenced groups such as indigenous communities now have unprecedented opportunities to make their voices heard. In Australia, for example, when the Aboriginal cause for land rights was ignored by the federal government, indigenous people went to the International Court of Human Rights and found a voice (even though the Court's determination is not binding on the Australian government).

Social work, with its mission to gain social justice and human rights and wellbeing for all and its experience working with oppressed groups, is in a unique position to work in partnership with vulnerable and disadvantaged people to strengthen their voices and restore some balance to the debates, thus working towards globalisation from below. Robert Polack (2004) suggests many ways by which social workers can contribute to globalisation from below, including teaching about globalisation and international social work in all social work courses. He concludes his review of social work's possible role this way:

> To put it directly, within our profession there is a wealth of experience, and accumulated knowledge base, and superior skills, which may be used in the service of empowering those who are exploited in the global economy. Social workers should work both collectively, in coalition with related organizations, and individually to effect change in the debt crisis and related global issues (Polack 2004: 289).

The challenge

These new definitions of social justice and human rights, incorporating individuals, groups and communities, address past criticisms that social work codes of ethics are only about individual clients. The IFSW definition and newer national codes (AASW 2000; NASW 1999; BASW 2002) are clear that human rights and human dignity and social justice is a general social issue for social workers, not to be limited to their work with individual clients. This poses a serious challenge to social work to put its rhetoric into practice.

In the face of the shrinking services to disadvantaged peoples, the rise of structural oppression and ever-increasing gaps between the advantaged and disadvantaged (that is, the rise of globalisation and with it neo-liberalism), social work has been strangely silent. Authors such as Gary Craig (2002) have noted that this recent silence is partly due to social workers having to cope with enormous workloads as a result of the reorganisation of welfare, their new roles as budget managers, and the downgrading of their positions, factors making up the challenges to social work discussed in earlier chapters. However, this silence is also a direct contravention of the more recent national and international codes of ethics.

On one hand writers such as Ife (2001) and Reichert (2003) argue that human rights frameworks can empower social work to achieve its goals and reinvigorate our understanding of social justice. Ife also argues that social work is in a unique position to help make the vision of human rights a reality. On the other hand, writers such as Cynthia Bisman (2004) argue that this lack of 'appropriate challenge' by social work 'amidst this sea of crises' is evidence of social work's low commitment to its value base, despite the widespread belief that values are central to social work. In its rush to prove that it is a 'real' profession, Bisman contends, social work has concentrated on developing its scientific knowledge and technical expertise, losing sight of its moral base in general, and social justice in particular. 'Without this emphasis on social justice', Bisman writes, 'there is little need if any, for social work or social workers' (2004: 115).

Clearly a commitment to human rights and human dignity, and to social justice, is needed if social work is to become empowered to act in partnership with disadvantaged peoples to fight for globalisation from below. Such a commitment has to be made with clear understanding and analysis of the complexities of these terms and how they can be interpreted from within particular discourses to favour certain groups and interests. For example, social work must resist the pressure to define human rights as only first-generation rights, and social justice as only equality of opportunity and procedural fairness. Similarly Pakulski, in discussing the 'third way' program, notes what has happened to notions of social equality under globalisation: 'Perhaps most importantly, social equality is redefined as equal freedom, equal treatment and equal opportunity rather than equal resourcing' (Pakulski 2004: 145). In contrast, social workers need to join forces with voices such as those of Gary Craig (2002: 670–1), who argues that: 'the goal of social justice requires that government confronts the inequities of market systems' and that equality of outcomes is a much better indicator of social justice than equality of opportunity.

Social work's current silence in the face of growing global inequality and shrinking welfare resources can to a large degree be understood as evidence that it has become entrapped in neo-liberalism, without being aware of its own capture. Thus many if not most social workers are powerfully invited by neo-liberalism to avoid responsibility for social justice and global issues, and to remain focused on their own individual clients who they in turn view as being largely responsible for their own condition. Without a clear analysis of globalisation, neo-liberalism and its particular understanding of the individual, social work codes fall prey to being interpreted from within the neo-liberal framework.

Virtues

In this chapter we have explored the purpose of social work by examining in some detail the two ethical principles laid down in the IFSW (2004) *Ethics in Social Work, Statement of Principles*. We have maintained throughout the book that commitment to particular virtues is the third foundation of the telos of social work, and that many of these are expressed in the twelve guidelines for professional conduct, also in the IFSW document. In this chapter, we remind social workers that they cannot practise ethically unless they incorporate the virtue of empathy into their work. This virtue is listed along with compassion and care in the fourth guideline for professional conduct in the IFSW statement.

Empathy is a skill and a virtue. It is about being able to 'walk in the shoes' of another, to understand both the content and the feelings they are experiencing, and to be able to communicate that understanding back to the person (Perry 1993). It is not clear from the case study whether Phoebe had an empathic understanding of the Williams family or not. The only way of knowing would be to see what the Williams' thought of their contact with Phoebe. What is clear is that without empathy with those with whom they work, social workers will not be effective in their quest for human rights or social justice.

Check your country's social work code for the list of standards of conduct that are set down as minimum standards for you to meet in your practice.

Ethical skills

Social workers need to practise the skill of self-awareness if they are to become ethical practitioners. If we are to critically analyse how we understand ethical principles such as human rights and social justice, and to recognise the impact of dominant discourses such as neo-liberalism, we need the self-awareness to acknowledge our own assumptions and prejudices.

Similarly, if we are to work in truly respectful partnerships that allow for diversity, we must be able to recognise our own values, prejudices and beliefs, and be able to set them to one side when necessary. The first step in this process is recognising what our beliefs and attitudes are. Social work can be described as an art and a science. Part of the art is a commitment to become ever more self-aware of our own barriers to really appreciating the other person's perspective. We do not know the basis for Phoebe's assessment that the Williams family will never be autonomous, nor what her own reactions to the family might have been. By presenting her opinions in the quasi-objective language of assessment, Phoebe does not identify the sources of her information nor how she arrived at her conclusions. A more empowering approach would be to be explicit about these things, and to acknowledge what has influenced her thinking. Of great importance is the Williams' attitude to her decisions and recommendations—something that is not included at this stage.

Ethical knowledge

In this chapter, we have argued that social workers require detailed knowledge of the ethical principles underpinning their own code of ethics, and of the *Ethics in Social Work, Statement of Principles* (IFSW 2004), to which most countries are signatories. In particular, social workers must be clear what they mean by human rights and human dignity and social justice. Not only should we draw on the knowledge of other disciplines such as philosophy, sociology and political science to broaden our understanding of these terms, we must contribute to the debates about it in other fields. With its central commitment to human rights and social justice and experience with disadvantaged people, social work is in an ideal position to provide leadership in these areas.

If Phoebe had explicitly referred to the IFSW *Statement of Principles* she may have taken quite a different stance in relation to the Williams family. She could have examined their strengths as well as areas of need, and focused on working in partnership with them to develop some options to present at the case conference. With a stronger emphasis on self-determination, participation and empowerment, the Williams' perspectives, even if different from Phoebe's, could have been considered as part of the discussion. Phoebe may also have used the statement or her own code of ethics to deepen her understanding of social justice, and to think about how her professional commitment to this principle fitted with the department's strategy. Finally, drawing on her communication skills, research and ability to work collectively, Phoebe would have done her homework about the services available in the wider community, and had a clearer understanding of resources and gaps and what role the department could take. Perhaps she could have linked the family to a greater range of resources such as literacy programs, or to other groups and services seeking to raise socio-economic conditions. Perhaps she could have argued that the family suffered discrimination as a result of being disadvantaged and so needed additional resources beyond the usual scope of the department. Acting as a sole agent, Phoebe is limited in what she can do to improve the circumstances. She requires a broader vision and range of strategies, and to work collectively with her colleagues to identity the causes of inequality and to work towards improved conditions, if both conditions for the Williams family and long-term objectives of social justice are to be achieved.

Conclusion

In this chapter we have argued that together, the two foundation ethical principles outlined in the IFSW statement have the potential to

re-invigorate and challenge social work to return to its roots of responding to exploitation and promoting human wellbeing. However if social
work is to become a significant voice for human wellbeing and social
justice, there is a great deal of work to be done. One of the tasks we must
undertake, in order to reclaim social work as a moral enterprise with
ethics as its driving force, is to sort out what we mean by human rights
and human dignity, and social justice, and to develop a shared understanding of these complex terms.

The ability of the profession to achieve its twin objectives will
continue to be beyond the capacity of individual social workers and the
profession in general unless social work codes of ethics are re-examined
and debated and the values and the underlying political philosophy that
inform the social work project made explicit. If this does not occur social
workers will continue their silence in the face of growing injustice. The
commitment to human rights and human dignity and social justice,
defined in terms of minimising social exclusion, social inequality, as well
as addressing systems and structures of domination and oppression, can
only be achieved through promoting social structures and patterns of
interaction that promote social relationships based on respect for the
intrinsic and equal value of each person as a member of society.

In this chapter we have identified empathy as a key virtue that social
workers must cultivate, if they are to practise ethically, along with
the need to develop the skill of self-awareness. When social workers
combine empathic understanding of others' situations alongside a
growing self-awareness, they will be in a much better position to
appreciate and support peoples' diversity as they join the struggle for
human rights and dignity and social justice in our world.

Study tasks

1   Study your social work code of ethics. Does it contain the three
    aspects of social work codes identified in this chapter:

a. commitment to human rights and human dignity,
b. commitment to social justice,
c. commitment to particular virtues and standards of professional conduct?

2   How does your code address human rights and human dignity? Does it include the elements listed in the IFSW statement? Are there other aspects of human rights and human dignity included that do not appear in the IFSW statement?

3   Consider the apparent conflict between individual and collective rights that was discussed in this chapter. Does your code of ethics preference one over the other?

4   How is social justice understood in your code of ethics? Is there an implication that its application is limited to work with clients, or is it applied more generally to the wider world? Are the five elements from the IFSW definition of social justice incorporated in your country's code?

5   What experience do you have of social workers working to promote human rights, human dignity and social justice at local, national or international levels?

6   As you develop your professional self, how can you build your skills of self-awareness and the virtue of empathy?

Further reading

Bowring, W. 2002, 'Forbidden Relations? The UK's Discourse of Human Rights and the Struggle for Social Justice', *Social Justice and Global Development Journal (LGD)* 2002(1) <http>//www2.warwick.ac.uk/fac/soc/law/elj/lgd/220_1/bowring/>. This lecture by Professor Bill Bowring discusses the relationship between human rights and social justice in the UK and how they are being reinterpreted under Labour's 'third way'.

Brecher, J., Costello, T. and Smith, B. 2002, 'Globalization and its Specter', in *Globalization from Below: The power of solidarity* (2nd edn), South End Press, Cambridge, Massachussets, pp. 1–17. This chapter provides a good summary of the forces of globalisation from above and below and explores some of the contradictions and complexities associated with globalisation from below.

Craig, G. 2002, 'Poverty, Social Work and Social Justice', *British Journal of Social Work*, vol. 32, no. 6, pp. 669–82. Provides a useful discussion of what social justice means, before exploring in detail how social justice is treated under New Labour in Britain and the implications for social work. Even if you are not interested in the British situation, the introduction to social justice and discussion about social work are worthwhile.

Ife, J. 2000, 'Community-based Options for Social Work: Sites for creative practice', in I. O'Connor, P. Smyth and J. Warburton (eds), *Contemporary Perspectives on Social Work and the Human Services: Challenges and change*, Longman, Sydney. An Australian perspective on how social justice and human rights are at the heart of social work.

Ife, J. 2001, *Human Rights and Social Work: Towards rights-based practice*, Cambridge University Press, Cambridge. In this practical and theoretical book Ife explores the issues for social work as a human rights-based profession from an internationalist perspective. Clearly written and with lots of practical examples, this is a must for social work students wanting to understand how human rights can inform social work practice.

Polack, R. 2004, 'Social Justice and the Global Economy: New challenges for social work in the 21st century', *Social Work*, vol. 49, no. 2, pp. 281–90. A North American perspective on social work's mandate to engage with globalisation and fight for social justice on a global level. Compelling statistics on the effects of increasing global inequalities, and some useful strategies for individual social workers as well as the social work profession as a whole.

Reichert, E. 2003, *Social Work and Human Rights: A foundation for policy and practice*, Columbia University Press, New York. Particularly relevant to North America, this book argues that human rights should be integrated into social work practice systematically and that the idea of human rights offers a framework for understanding social work principles.

Thompson, N. 2002, 'Social Movements, Social Justice and Social Work', *British Journal of Social Work*, vol. 32, no. 6, pp. 711–22. A clear discussion from a British perspective on social justice, social movements and social work and how social work needs to work with social movements and other oppressed groups in partnerships.

Wissenburg, M. 1999, *Imperfection and Impartiality*, UCL Press, London. From the Netherlands, this book explores the changing nature of liberalism, including a discussion of its impact on social justice.

Websites

United Nations website on human rights <http://www.un.org/rights/>. A clearing house of information on the Universal Declaration of Human Rights, and other treaties and instruments enumerating the various human rights recognised by the United Nations.

Part three
Social work ethics in practice

6
Autonomy, paternalism and self-determination

Two social workers are walking along a beach, engrossed in their conversation. They notice a man in the surf waving his arms as he goes under the water. The two social workers resume their conversation and keep on walking. They look up again, and see the man still waving his arms before he goes under the surface once more.

'I wonder if he is in difficulty?' one social worker says to the other. They walk on further. Finally, the man shouts out, 'Help me, please!' whereupon one of the social workers says to the other, 'At last—he is asking to become a client. Now we can rescue him.'

All professions have their jokes. Most emanate from within the professions themselves and many, by exaggeration, sarcasm, irony or whatever, mock the supposed character or characteristics of the particular profession in question or its members. As with many of these jokes there is an element, or at least a very small grain, of truth in the above example about the social work profession. So, what might this mildly amusing joke be saying about the social work profession or about social workers?

In all probability what the joke is alluding to is the importance social work and social workers attach to client autonomy and self-determination and the client's desire to change, including exercising choice about entering into some kind of relationship with the social worker. The joke attempts to capture an idealisation of the social work

relationship—voluntary and consensual—although in reality many
people have no such choices.

Let us change the story to make it more realistic.

Norika Pawar and Gina Boetto are two social workers in the Aged
Care Assessment Team (ACAT). One Monday morning, Gina took a
call from a Mrs Parker, who lives in a unit on a public housing estate.
She stated that she had not seen Mary Moxham for a number of
days and wondered if 'social services' could help. Gina told Mrs
Parker that she will follow it up. Norika, the senior social worker, said
to Gina, 'That will be "Scary Mary"—we had a call about her six
months ago after someone said, it might have been Mrs Parker, she
was getting harassed by a local gang of teenagers on the estate.
We offered her a range of services, including the chance to be
rehoused, but she refused. Your predecessor, who tried to interview
her, was given very short shrift when she called on her and was told
to mind her own business. She found her quite alarming. Look Gina,
leave this with me, and I will follow it up later, but we better get to
that case conference that started five minutes ago.'

A week later, Gina read a newspaper report of a woman found
dead in her unit on the same housing estate. Neighbours had
complained to the local council about the smell, and the police had
forced the front door to gain entry. According to the report, an
elderly woman was found sitting slumped in an armchair near the
kitchen table. The kitchen was described as 'squalid', with
unwashed crockery, rotting food, piles of rubbish and a large
number of cats climbing over the table, sink and other work
surfaces.

Alarm bells rang in Gina's mind so she contacted the local
police, who told her the dead woman was a Mrs Moxham. They
also mentioned they might need to speak with someone in the
ACAT, because they had a statement from a Mrs Parker claiming
she contacted them nearly a week ago about Mrs Moxham.

Gina asked Norika if she ever did anything about the original call. Norika replied, 'It did slip my mind and when I did remember I thought there was little point in a follow up because of the way she carried on last time.'

The circumstances surrounding Mary Moxham's death are now the subject of a coronial inquiry, and Gina and Norika have been called to give evidence.

Cases where a self-neglecting older person becomes socially isolated and their health and wellbeing suffers to the point where they are at physical risk of serious harm, including death, epitomise the problems and ethical challenges sometimes faced by social workers. The person's isolation makes it difficult for the worker to even know what is happening. In many jurisdictions mere suspicion that someone might be vulnerable to harm is not enough to justify intervention unless there is evidence to support action under either mental health or adult guardianship laws. Even if it is clear what is happening, many professionals may still feel unable to act (intervene), or at least to justify why they are acting (intervening).

In this chapter and the next, we consider the ways in which the principles of autonomy, privacy, client self-determination and the problem of paternalism affect social work practice. However, before we do so, it is necessary to consider if professional social workers have some general ethical duty to help. This might seem a surprising question to ask as many would assume that social workers do, but it is by no means certain.

Is there a duty to help?

Do social workers have an ethical duty to render aid and assistance to those who are vulnerable and if they do, where does that duty come from and what is its scope? A good starting point is your country's social work code of ethics.

The Australian Association of Social Workers (AASW 2000) code, as an example, reflects the professional pluralism found in many professional social work codes and it maintains a strong focus on relations with clients (as one might expect). While the code makes a strong commitment to the ideal and the pursuit of social justice, respect for human dignity, professional integrity and practice competence, trying to find a clear statement of commitment to help and render aid to the vulnerable is less easy to find.

From the AASW code we might divine a commitment to help from statements about 'respect for clients' and 'preserving and promoting dignity'. Within the definition of a 'duty of care', which is not the same as a duty *to* care, a reference to 'the duty of people in particular circumstances and occupations to protect and control others' might indicate a general duty to aid. However, virtually all the obligations and duties of social workers are expressed in relation to clients. In the world of the neglected and the self-neglecting, like the elderly woman in our scenario, people are often not yet clients—they may still need to be 'discovered' or identified. Social workers are only enjoined to protect the privacy of clients, 'taking care not to intrude unnecessarily on clients' privacy when seeking information'. But invading privacy, both spatial and informational, is precisely what social workers and others must do sometimes in order to render aid to the vulnerable. We will return to this point in chapter 7. Suffice to say, it is quite conceivable that when applying the AASW code of ethics to our modified scenario above, the two social workers could comfortably justify doing nothing, by saying: 'the woman is not a client and previously refused our offers of help'; 'we didn't want to invade her privacy'; 'we are respecting her dignity and worth because she has not given her informed consent to services' (i.e. for purposeful intervention such as an ambulance or medical assistance).

On that interpretation of the code, and given the social workers could claim no real guidance from the code as to whether they ought to have acted or not, perhaps they stand in no special relationship and owe no duties to anybody other than those who are their clients. Perhaps they stand in relation to the vulnerable in the same way that any stranger does—they can just walk away with no legal or moral opprobrium being heaped on them.

Commonsense morality and/or ethical intuition, as well as the emotional response to a person seen to be in distress, suggest some kind of 'rescue' is needed. In the case of a person trapped in a burning house we have no problem accepting that something ought to be done, but a self-neglecting person 'trapped' in their house is one of those problematic cases that seems to engender a kind of ethical paralysis, partly because professional ethical principles seem unable to help—the presumed personal choice of the 'victim' to be left alone and not seek help is often seen to trump any other obligation the worker might think they have to help.

We are not seriously suggesting that social workers have general duties to 'help' all those in need—that would be impossible and unreasonable. In general, social workers have the same 'duty of rescue' shared by other people. Social workers will always have to make choices about who they help and in what circumstances. But what we are saying is that if ethical practice is the core of what it is to be a good social worker, then social workers cannot hide behind their ethical principles or use the principles as trumps in ways that effectively undermine or even negate their raison d'être.

Autonomy versus paternalism

Social workers cannot avoid getting their hands dirty and they cannot get squeamish about the professional ethical choices they might have to make because their daily practice often requires them to make decisions that have an impact on their clients' autonomy. This can occur directly as a result of a casework decision, or indirectly through the development of a new policy or procedure. While many such decisions may be made with a view to promoting client autonomy, they can also limit it. This is particularly so in the field of statutory social work involving the exercise of paternalistic decision-making.

While the promotion of autonomy may be the most desirable outcome for a client, there are occasions when clients are unable to act in their own best interests and coercion and interference are justified. Thus, in order to practice effectively social workers require an understanding of autonomy, paternalism, the social work concept of self-determination and how the three concepts separately and in combination can be applied for the benefit of clients.

First, a note of caution. As with the terms 'human rights' and 'social justice', notions of autonomy and paternalism are first and foremost social constructs. That is, they give very particular expressions to more fundamental interests, expressions dependent on certain social contexts for their meaning. These values change over time, and different interest groups hold varying interpretations of them in the present. In this regard, and acknowledging the manner in which the political discourse frequently subjugates other ways of interpreting these terms, social workers need to have a very clear understanding of the meaning given to 'autonomy' and 'paternalism' in different discourses and the consequences of integrating such terms and their meanings, without questioning them, into the social work discourse.

Clark (2000: 24) suggests that the social work profession 'shares the widespread value of individual autonomy', meaning how it is understood in the wider community and therefore the political discourse. Reflecting Clark's view that social workers have accepted the common meaning of autonomy as self-rule, there is little evidence in the social work literature of the term being debated or explored by social workers. Rather, it would seem that autonomy is a received idea that social work has acquired unquestioningly without a full understanding of the implications. This is a good example of the way in which practice can define theory.

While autonomy is not specifically identified as a social work value it would appear, in practice, to be one by default, being received from the liberal tradition along with the related values of freedom, justice and community (Clark 2000), although the standing of the last is being challenged by contemporary neo-liberal ideology. Autonomy can be obstructed by others, by their action or inaction, and by the person's incapacity or failure to adequately care for themselves. A social worker can threaten a client's autonomy by proposing a course of action that is contrary to the client's wishes (Clark 2000). In order to avoid interfering with the autonomy of their clients, some social workers seek to adopt a position of neutrality with regard to values and standards by practising what Clark (2000: 164) calls '[social] agnosticism'. As an example, the two social workers in our case study demonstrated social agnosticism when they did not respond to the neighbour's call. By giving priority to this interpretation of autonomy, social workers abrogate their responsibility to other principles inherent in codes of ethics such as respecting the dignity and worth of the whole person and working towards social justice.

Autonomy

When social workers talk about autonomy, it is usually with regard to clients within particular practice contexts and in relation to their taking specific decisions and actions. As an example, within the mental health field, a voluntary patient or client who chooses to cease psychotherapy or to take medication may be regarded as exercising their autonomy. By comparison, it is unusual to hear discussions about client autonomy within child protection. However, in both areas, the key element is that autonomy concerns individual clients in taking specific decisions or taking particular courses of action. This represents a very limited interpretation and application of autonomy and may even involve abdication of responsibility by the worker.

So what is autonomy if it is not about individual decisions taken by clients? As a starting point we prefer seeing autonomy as a notion relating to the total being and life circumstances of a person, not just isolated choices. This is in tune with the IFSW's (2004) *Ethics in Social Work, Statement of Principles* that includes as the third element of respecting human rights and human dignity:

Treating each person as a whole—social workers should be

concerned with the whole person, within the family, community and societal and natural environments, and should seek to recognise all aspects of a person's life.

Indeed, the notion of autonomy seems to underpin the entire first fundamental principle listed in the IFSW statement—respect for human rights and human dignity—which is expressed as:

> Social workers should uphold and defend each person's physical, psychological, emotional and spiritual integrity and well-being.

As noted in chapter 5, this principle is not restricted to clients; it is expressed as social workers' obligations to all people. The four elements included in this principle are people's rights to self-determination, to participate in the decisions and actions of social workers, to be treated as a whole (as above) and to have their strengths identified and developed.

Like social justice, autonomy is unusual in being both a political and an ethical value. Initially a feature of Victorian British liberalism, autonomy has been incorporated into all political discourses informed by liberalism. However, it is worth noting that it has a more restricted interpretation in liberal societies in the English-speaking (Anglo-American) western world than it has in the non-English speaking countries of Western Europe. Within Anglo-American countries the culture of liberal individualism 'has extended the rights of the autonomous individual as the dominant ideology' (Clark 2000: 97), whereas in Europe the interpretation of autonomy is informed more by social democratic values that see the person embedded in their community.

Autonomy relies on two conditions: both the capacity of the person to be autonomous, and the social provision of the resources and opportunities to exercise this capacity. Wissenburg (1999) defines autonomy as freedom of mind, limited only by the capacity of each person to reason and act rationally. If a person's ability to think rationally is limited in some way, so is their capacity for autonomy. This casts some doubt on the capacity of the voluntary patient mentioned above, who ceased taking their medication, to exercise autonomy, if the decision was not a rational one. Because autonomy is based on the capacity to exercise rational thought it is subject to a great deal of individual variation, rather than being absolute.

In addition, autonomy does not mean doing as one likes and acting independently of the wellbeing of society. The conditions for autonomy demand social institutions, practices and structures, such as families to rear us, schools to educate us, and systems for verifying the truth of what we are told. In exercising autonomy each person has to sustain these conditions by having regard to rules, both statutory and moral, that govern society (Rawls 1971). Put another way, 'without rules and reasons we cannot in any way be autonomous . . . let alone rational' (Wissenburg 1999: 70). Thus, autonomy of thought and action is based on the capacity of each person to reason and act in a rational and objective manner (Wissenburg 1999; Rawls 1971).

Autonomy is also conditional upon the capacity to act without being compromised by influence or coercion and so derives from a 'well ordered society' (Rawls 1971: 520). However, it is not a one-sided equation as the greater the degree of autonomy exercised by a person, the greater their responsibility to themselves and the people they interact with (van Berkel and Moller 2002). This responsibility extends, by implication, to social institutions and government. A person has to be in a culture that allows them to choose whether to exercise their autonomy. Such a decision should not be imposed, but self-willed. In some instances there may be a need for government to intervene in the operation of the market to ensure the equitable distribution of resources sufficient to enable people to be autonomous (Gray 1995). In previous chapters we have made a similar argument for government intervention in the market to foster social justice and human rights. On the other hand, government can intervene in ways that reduce autonomy. For example, the Australian government has proposed making the provision of limited financial assistance to an indigenous community conditional upon the community keeping their children clean, adequately clothed and at school (Metherell and Gauntlett 2004).

Autonomy cannot be considered on its own, only as one of a package of liberal values (Bellamy 1992). Being an extension of the liberal notion of freedom from harm and freedom from interference in self-actualisation (Rooney 1992), it is expressed in a number of different ways. One is a libertarian version, which implies freedom from paternalistic state intervention and support, conditional and restricted social welfare assistance and seeing the individual as being responsible for their own acts (van Berkel and Moller 2002). In this context basic rights consist of judicial protection, freedom from coercion, freedom of association and movement, civil liberties and economic freedom (Gray 1995). Another view of autonomy, sometimes called welfare liberalism, is advocated by Rawls (1996). This view includes the provision of a basket of basic goods that include education, health care, income and self-respect, liberty, justice and being able to participate in the affairs of society (Rawls 1996).

Neo-liberal society relies on the libertarian version of autonomy, emphasising the individual at the expense of community, reliance upon market forces to structure social relations, and a residual role for the state that excludes the state from mediating the more adverse effects of the market upon people. Taking a more market-oriented approach Gray (1995) suggests that a central feature of liberal autonomy is the ownership of private property. By comparison, people whose only resource is their labour and their only assets the wages they earn are considered to be less autonomous than those with property. However, participation in the marketplace does not necessarily promote autonomy, as the market can be oppressive and require individuals to act in certain ways, such as in being required to exchange their labour for goods. This led Agger (1992) to suggest that under the present political discourse autonomy has been replaced by conformity.

Despite the dominance of libertarian ideas, autonomy can also enhance social inclusion by dismantling structures of oppression. In doing so each person is encouraged to utilise their capacities, subject to their being sufficiently resourced to meet their basic needs. However, like autonomy, the provision of resources to enable social inclusion should not be conditional upon people being required to meet particular criteria (van Berkel and Moller 2002) such as 'work for the welfare' programs.

Paternalism

Paternalism is often thought of as the opposite of autonomy, a negation of the subject's ability to exercise their autonomy. Like autonomy, paternalism is individualised in its application. While there is no agreement on the meaning of paternalism, Reamer (2001: 109) observed that the central element is 'the use of coercion or interference that is justified by concern for the good of the individual who is coerced or interfered with'.

According to Clark (2000), paternalism is a pluralistic construct, having multiple expressions. Clark speaks of private paternalism, as exercised by a person who prevents another from attempting suicide. This he contrasted with public or legal paternalism in which the state, through legislation, restricts access to some activities, such as dangerous sports (bungy jumping), or makes other activities conditional, such as the need to wear a seat belt when travelling in a vehicle. The other distinction Clark made was between direct paternalism, which benefits the person being restricted, for example, as exercised by a parent over a child, and indirect paternalism, which restricts some people's freedom to benefit others. Examples include legislation passed in order to protect some or all of the public from self-harming behaviours, e.g. making it illegal to sell cigarettes to minors. A further example is occupational health and safety legislation that imposes responsibilities upon employers to intervene in the work practices of their employees to prevent self-harm arising out of unsafe work practices.

By comparison, Dworkin (2002) suggests paternalism is a unitary construct, but with a number of overlapping dimensions. It can be hard or soft, and broad or narrow, and weak or strong, and pure or impure, and moral or welfare-oriented. Soft paternalism restricts intervention to only those situations in which a person, having sufficient knowledge and acting from a position that is coercion free, invites intervention whereas hard paternalism, which can only be justified in the extreme, prevents a person from attempting suicide. Narrow paternalism is limited to the use of legal coercion by the state, whereas broad paternalism is concerned with any paternalistic action, no matter how it occurs, by whom or the degree of significance of the interference. Weak paternalism is limited to intervening in the means a person may employ to achieve a particular end when it is apparent that the means are inappropriate or bound to fail. By comparison, strong paternalism justifies interference with the ends or outcomes sought by a person when it can be shown that the sought end or outcome is mistaken or is not the end or outcome that the person would rationally choose. Welfare paternalism, however, is based on a concern for the physical and psychological wellbeing of a person or persons. Moral paternalism is not, in the first instance, concerned with a person's physical and psychological wellbeing. Rather such interference reflects social values that certain behaviours are degrading and/or morally wrong, even though they may be voluntarily entered into. Examples include prohibiting prostitution, witchcraft, adultery, blasphemy and homosexuality.

As can be seen, many elements of moral paternalism are closely linked with some religious values. However, no matter how it is constructed, paternalism revolves around the extent to which the person is considered to be a danger to him or herself. Most people accept the need for coercion and interference in the life of a person if they are satisfied that the person is unable to arrange their own affairs. While ambivalent about such intervention, society demands of the state a degree of paternalism when it is considered a person cannot look after their own interests and, in the absence of intervention, may harm themselves. Examples include aspects of child protection legislation, particularly involving sexual abuse and paedophilia, as children are among the most powerless in society; and people with disabilities and those with mental health problems that affect their capacity to look after themselves and to act in their own best interests. The detention of the criminally insane is yet another example of paternalism as on occasions extreme measures are required to protect a person from themselves (as well as protecting society). Other examples of paternalism include public health laws governing food standards and hygiene, the reporting of communicable diseases and the requirement that cyclists and motorcycle riders wear helmets.

Paternalism becomes harder to justify the less incapacitated a person is to manage their affairs. Reamer (2001) suggests that social workers should not intervene unless clients pose a risk or severe threat to themselves. (This is not to disregard the threat some people can pose to others, as with domestic violence, but intervention in such situations does not necessarily constitute paternalism.) Paternalism becomes increasingly justified the more a client is unable to promote their autonomy. While behaving in a paternalistic manner means constraining a person's autonomy, in many instances the autonomy forgone will be consistent with the extent to which the person is unable to exercise that autonomy. However, the justifiable use of paternalism does not obviate the need for transparency. Just because a client forgoes or is forced to forgo their autonomy for whatever reason, it does not mean they forgo their right to have explained to them or their representative the reasons why their autonomy is being denied them and to have their rights of appeal and review explained.

Paternalism has become a pejorative term, a dirty word. This, though, ignores the fact that it is through paternalism that autonomy is achieved. Focusing on the negative connotations of paternalism can lead us to ignore the positive aspects, particularly when it is used to assist individuals to develop the skills that lead to their becoming autonomous. The best example of this is the paternalism exercised by parents over children, a paternalism that is initially all-encompassing but is progressively reduced as the child gets older and develops the capacity to understand and reason through the acquisition of knowledge and experience. One of the mistakes some parents make is to grant their children too much autonomy too early, leading to a range of social and relational problems that can result in the state intervening to limit the child's autonomy. This notion of diminishing paternalism and increasing autonomy is reflected in a range of legislation that regulates the affairs of children.

Similar provisions can be found for adults unable to manage their affairs. Many jurisdictions have laws that enable either the decisions concerning a person's total or partial guardianship to be taken by another. This can be limited to an aspect of the person's affairs, such as managing or protecting their finances, through to taking all decisions on their behalf. Clark (2000) suggests that the criteria for justifying paternalistic intervention involve a demonstrated risk of harm by the person to themselves, a lack of knowledge and understanding and, in particular, the inability to give informed consent.

In a very practical sense the question arises about the extent to which social workers can promote their clients' autonomy, or even their own professional autonomy. This situation occurs as most social workers are employees, rather than self-employed. As such they are required to adhere to their conditions of employment, an agency code of ethics and a range of policies, procedures and statutory requirements. They may not even practise in their own right, but as a delegate of an official who has a statutory responsibility. A social worker employed in a paternalistic environment is characterised by having limited authority and discretion to act in their own right and restricted to following a set of directions.

Statutory requirements can deny a client their autonomy, and the ability of a social worker to promote the client's autonomy. As an example, under certain circumstances a person can lose the right to refuse medication or the right to deny a worker access to their home, as is the case in child protection investigations. While workers may have little choice in such instances, they still have some discretion over the way in which they approach individual clients. Even though a client's autonomy may be set aside, they do not have to also be disempowered in their interactions with others.

Self-determination

Bridging the values of autonomy and paternalism is self-determination. The IFSW (2004) statement refers to self-determination as:

respect[ing] and promot[ing] people's rights to make their own choices and decisions, irrespective of their values and life choices, provided this does not threaten the rights and legitimate interests of others.

The concept of self-determination clearly promotes autonomy and yet can still be applied within a paternalistic framework. This can be achieved by involving the client in all decision-making, to the extent of their ability, even if the final decision does not rest with them. This concept has long been one of social work's core values and is probably the oldest social work value. Thus it comes as no surprise that all social work codes of ethics either explicitly or implicitly acknowledge the need to promote autonomy, while at the same time recognising that paternalism can be justified, and then walk the middle path by promoting self-determination, which can accommodate both autonomy and paternalism (Banks 2001). By making sure clients understand their 'rights' and are assisted to make informed decisions, they can still be self-determining, albeit with a limited scope.

Rooney (1992), a social worker, while differentiating between autonomy and self-determination, also speaks of a relationship in which self-determination is a prerequisite to autonomy. He also differentiates between positive and negative self-determination. Negative self-determination is the ability to think and act without duress or coercion, to be free from harm. By comparison, positive self-determination is achieved when a person has the knowledge, skills and resources to pursue self-identified goals. Such values are reflective of core liberal values, further suggesting that social work in the English-speaking world is framed by the political discourse of liberalism.

Even within a paternalistic environment, by assisting a client to be more self-determining autonomy can be encouraged. This can be achieved through the worker-client relationship, rather than the application of a prescribed set of policies and procedures. It is the nature of the casework relationship that the social worker can include or exclude the client from information about the decision-making process and the actual taking of decisions. In such situations, while client autonomy may not be a viable option and a measure of coercion and interference justified, within the framework provided by the casework relationship client self-determination can be promoted.

The law also provides some good examples of self-determination, although their implementation may require some advocacy. Consistent with their age and developmental capacity, children progressively acquire responsibilities and rights at law. While this may not promote their autonomy, it does enable them to progressively become more self-determining until they reach their majority and, in most cases, become legally autonomous. Concurrently, the responsibilities of parents are progressively reduced, reflecting the principle of diminishing parental control. While there are variations across jurisdictions in and across different countries, the basic theme of increasing responsibility, rights and autonomy and diminishing paternalism holds good. Thus, in Australia, at age ten children are held responsible for any criminal acts they may commit, even if the penalties are different to those imposed upon adults and juveniles. At age 12 children have a right to be heard and have their views considered in divorce proceedings, particularly in matters of custody. Boys and girls at age 16 can lawfully consent to sexual relations with members of the opposite sex and can legally leave home (some can do this at age 15) (*NSW Law Handbook* 2005). At age 16 children in many jurisdictions are regarded as young persons and can enter into contracts in their own right. At age 17 they can legally drive a vehicle, while at 18 they are regarded as adults, can join the armed forces, smoke and enter places where alcohol is served and consume intoxicating spirits.

To conclude our earlier scenario involving the death of the elderly woman, during the inquiry into her death the actions or inactions of the two social workers came under considerable scrutiny and criticism and three key themes emerged. First, what might be the ethical justification, if any, for intervening in the lives of individuals, particularly when they are not even social work clients? Second, the importance of differentiating autonomy and self-determination. Third, the question of what makes a good social worker.

In its findings, the inquiry found that social workers, in virtue of their specialist training and their professional ethics, are not always able to separate out their private from their professional lives. In short, attached to the status of social worker are certain role responsibilities that the ordinary citizen does not have. Social workers may not always have the luxury of picking and choosing who they help and when. Moreover, social workers, like other professionals such as doctors and nurses, will always be judged for what they do or do not do, even in their personal lives, and particularly when they encounter situations that demand a professional response.

Social work practitioners have to accept that their interventions in the lives of others will always, by definition, impact on the autonomy of others. Sometimes their actions will, prima facie, be paternalistic and, by definition, those interventions could involve breaching privacy. However, it is hoped that those interventions could also allow a person to become more self-determining, to make better informed choices and to have better, more fulfilling lives. Whatever social workers choose to do, they cannot be ethically passive bystanders.

The inquiry rejected the social workers' argument that by doing nothing they were respecting the right of the woman not to become a client and not to have her privacy invaded, because in the inquiry's view something had to be done even if it was just to find out she did not need or want any help. Nor was the inquiry satisfied with the argument that their 'non-intervention' was respecting the dignity and self-worth of the elderly woman. The Coroner scathingly observed that 'there is nothing dignified in dying alone and in squalor!' Furthermore, the Coroner also observed there was a difference between intervention and non-intervention on the one hand, and simply doing nothing on the other. Professional intervention or non-intervention should involve the social worker exercising their professional skill and judgement, based on their knowledge, practice wisdom and a sound understanding of the ethical bases for their decisions. Doing nothing and then seeking to hide behind their ethical code undermined the very purpose for which they became social workers.

Virtues

You might think we are expecting social workers to be self-sacrificing moral heroes and that we are being unduly and unfairly harsh on the social workers in our scenario. We don't think we are. Our point is that social workers will always be exposed to situations involving hard choices and even moral and legal risk. Social workers also have to recognise that their professional lives inevitably involve making decisions that will impact on the lives and wellbeing of others in all sorts of ways.

Sometimes social workers will have to wear the charge that they are paternalistic or that they have undermined the autonomy of their clients. One way to walk this divide is to cultivate a commitment to social work values, as set out in your code of ethics, particularly as one of the more corrosive effects of bureaucratism and defensive practice has been the supplanting of professional codes of ethics with organisation-based generic codes of conduct. We term this commitment to social work values the virtue of integrity.

If the two social workers in our scenario had applied their profession's values and pondered why it was that Mary so adamantly rejected earlier offers of assistance rather than just assuming she would reject further offers, the outcome could have been very different. Taking the time to touch base with how clients feel is important in tracking how disempowering or alien their experience of care has become. The point we are making here is to stress the importance of cultivating a client focus and communication skills to engage with clients and walk a mile in their shoes.

Social workers need to remember that, in becoming a client, people are placing their trust in them. Mary, for example, may be surrendering a portion of her autonomy and so her ability to make her own choices about her life, albeit in the short term, for a promise that the social work intervention in her life will provide amelioration of her present condition. Maybe Mary was frightened to admit she felt unsafe where she was living, that she was not coping and able to care for herself as well as she used to. Whatever Mary's reasons, the application of social work values, and in particular empathy, might have allowed the social workers to move beyond what, in the end, turned out to be a dangerous assumption to thinking about who they might best engage with Mary to help her.

Ethical skills

The practice of ethics is an exercise of practical wisdom because it is about learning how to assess the elements of a dilemma and decide, all things considered, what one ought to do. Social workers don't inhabit a professional world of voluntary clients entering into consensual and equal relations. Their clients are often involuntary and unequal. It is naive to construct one's ethics as if we inhabit this idealised world. Clients might be unable to exercise full autonomy; their capacity to make choices and to physically and emotionally care for themselves may be impaired in some way—by age, disability or mental state.

One of the core values of social work is respect for (all) persons. However, it is one thing to value respect for itself, it is quite another to practise respect. Doing so involves being aware of both the person as an individual and community member and having regard for their social context. In doing so social workers are able to demonstrate and provide professional leadership that derives from social work values. They also demonstrate the value of a code of ethics and how it can be used to inform decisions in working with both clients and those who are not yet their clients and in demonstrating when they should intervene and when they should not. This skill involves learning a middle road between autonomy and paternalism—the road of fostering self-determination as discussed in this chapter. It involves knowing the limits of the professional role and, ultimately, being able to justify what they have done according to a set of articulated values.

Asking whether the elderly woman in the case study had the ability to be self-determining and, if not, what could be done to foster this might also have led to very different outcomes. The social workers involved did not even begin to attempt an assessment of the woman's state, nor whether she was able to make informed choices. They displayed no professional leadership. With their simplistic view of autonomy to justify their lack of action, they felt safe in ignoring a human tragedy.

Ethical knowledge

At the heart of social work is demonstrating respect for each person. Often this involves divining the right line to walk between autonomy and paternalism. This in turn requires an understanding of the commitments of your code of ethics. It also requires you to know the limits and possibilities of your particular work context. Practising respect for persons demands more than just the normal focus on what the rules don't allow or other limitations on practice. In our case study, having respect for persons means doing your best for them and being proactive. The proactive worker needs to dig deep into the regulations, rules, processes and laws that structure their work to find resources and opportunities for clients. While constant struggle and conflict are unproductive, you can make strategic decisions about when to chase things and when to push by referring to the framework of self-determination described above. If you chase after those things that will promote the client's capacity to exercise self-determination, and so enhance their respect, you can avoid working too hard and dissipating your energies while still working proactively for your clients.

Conclusion

In summary, there are conditions prerequisite to the exercise of autonomy. Further, as most people who become social work clients have an issue they are unable to manage themselves that impacts upon their capacity to be autonomous, the question arises as to whether it is realistic for social workers to speak of clients and autonomy. Add to this the power dimension involved in all social work relationships, in which the social worker, if for no other reason than their professional status, is regarded as the expert by the client or has authority over the client, one has to question if social workers can realistically speak of promoting a client's autonomy. In addition, is it realistic to speak of autonomy with regard to social work practice with children, people with disabilities, the dependent aged, the disadvantaged and those who are structurally oppressed, all of whom are among the most disempowered members of society?

The social work value of self-determination is a more achievable objective as it can be constructed within the context of specific issues and goals. In this context, providing a client with the opportunity to be self-determining involves acknowledging, but not necessarily accepting, nor encouraging the client to accept, structural limitations in their life and the limitations upon their capacity to make decisions on matters affecting them. While most social worker-client relationships cannot begin as a working partnership, we have discussed the importance of working towards partnership and a more equal relationship. Working towards this goal of partnership is an important element of fostering self-determination. Often this goal is only realised towards the end of the social worker–client relationship. Self-determination also involves ensuring that agency policies and procedures facilitate client participation, accommodate the client's special needs and circumstances and enable them to be accompanied to all meetings and sessions by a support person or even to have, if appropriate, a representative attend on their behalf. Facilitating self-determination also involves social workers having an awareness of and commitment to their code of ethics, of applying them and demonstrating ethical practice and so leading by example, and finally of practising respect for all persons they interact with.

Study tasks

1   Confronted with the circumstances our two social workers found themselves in, what would you have done? Do you think your

professional obligations require you to act in some way? How would you justify what you decide to do or not do, as the case may be?

2   What do you regard as the differences between intervention and non-intervention on the one hand, and simply doing nothing on the other?

3   Is it possible to justify paternalistic intervention?

4   What does self-determination mean to you? Compare your understanding with others in your group or class.

5   How do you react to the idea that as a social worker you have to see some things and cannot look away, even when you are not working?

6   How can you promote your professional autonomy when faced with an employment situation that restricts your capacity to act independently by imposing upon you restrictive decision-making models?

7   Do you think autonomy should be limited to those persons who have the capacity to take informed and rational decisions? Should paternalistic controls be limited to persons unable to take such decisions?

8   Think of different situations, such as aged care, child protection or mental health, and consider how you might demonstrate respect for persons and show professional leadership and a commitment to social work values.

Further reading

Clark, C. 2000, *Social Work Ethics, Politics, Principles and Practice*, Macmillan, London. Autonomy, paternalism and citizenship is dealt with in chapter 10.

Rathbone-McCuan, E. and Fabian, D.R. 1992, *Self-neglecting Elders: A clinical dilemma*, Auburn House, New York. One of the most comprehensive texts on self-neglecting elderly, including the ethical issues.

Reamer, F. 2001, *Social Work Values and Ethics*, Columbia, New York. Chapter 4 discusses self-determination and paternalism.

Rooney, R. 1992, *Strategies for Work with Involuntary Clients*, Columbia University Press, New York. Addresses issues of empowerment, autonomy, paternalism and self-determination.

Wicclair, M.R. 1993, *Ethics and the Elderly*, Oxford University Press, New York.

Website

Stanford Encyclopedia of Philosophy <http://setis.library.usyd.edu.au/stanford/entries/autonomy-moral/>. John Christman's entry on autonomy concentrates primarily on the political and philosophical aspects of the concept.

7
Privacy and confidentiality[1]

Case study 1

Jane is a social worker with the department of community services. She shares a flat with Mike Collins, a young, recently qualified solicitor who works for a suburban firm of lawyers. In his spare time he works for free at the local community centre, which is where he first met Jane. One evening, Mike tells her about a client he saw, how he has an uncomfortable feeling about it but can't quite put his finger on it.

A man came in to see Mike and said his wife had left him and taken the boys and he wanted to find out about custody and access proceedings. He believed she was living with the boys nearby, but he had no details. He explained that she had left after a very acrimonious argument. He admitted that he'd threatened her, but did not physically harm her. The husband explained that he was currently on sick leave from his job as a painter with the local council because he had broken his hand. He had got into a fight with someone at the pub over an international rugby match between Wales and Australia. 'I'm a Welshman, I like to drink and I take my rugby seriously. Because I have been at home a lot, getting under my wife's feet, we've been arguing more than usual.'

Mike explained the procedures for seeking custody and

---

[1] Parts of this chapter are reproduced and adapted from M. Collingridge, S. Miller and W. Bowles (2001).

access to the husband and said he would make some inquiries about the boys' whereabouts and suggested he came back to see him in a few days' time.

On hearing this, Jane immediately says, 'You're talking about the Davis family—I know them.' She tells Mike that Mrs Davis was currently in the local women's refuge with the boys and that it was a bit more than an 'acrimonious argument'.

Furthermore, says Jane, 'Although there is no suggestion this time that Mr Davis has harmed the boys, the school liaison office has notified the department in the past about the boys coming to school with unexplained bruises.'

The following morning Mike mentions the problem to his senior partner, who becomes extremely angry. He says that not only has Jane breached confidentiality by revealing the information about the family, she has compromised Mike's position with his client. He finishes by suggesting it is better not to know this type of unproven allegation about child mistreatment as it might cloud Mike's judgement. Mike protests that the information is vital as to how he eventually might advise his client, especially since he is seeking custody. However, the senior partner is unmoved. He warns Mike about his relationship with Jane. He points out that just because two professional people live together their respective clients do not forgo their confidentiality; the intimacy of the relationship does not override client confidentiality.

Mike contacts Mr Davis to postpone their next meeting. Mr Davis asks about his wife's whereabouts but Mike says he has no information.

Jane tells Mike that evening that the department will investigate the case even though there is no formal notification. She says she felt bound to act to protect the boys, even though the earlier allegations were vague and unproven. Mike agrees, but wonders if it might have been better if nothing had been said on either side, especially as he heard that afternoon that Mrs Davis and the boys have returned to the family home.

In this scenario, the problems of interpersonal relationships have become entangled with confidentiality as well as duties to act—in this case to investigate or report cases of child neglect and abuse. Maintaining professional separateness in interpersonal and inter-professional relationships is difficult, but lack of care in talking about cases and failing to take adequate steps to de-identify information has resulted in both professionals being placed in difficult, conflictual situations.

This scenario, like most of the case studies in the book, is based on real events modified to make a point. An added twist, and what actually happened, was that one of the authors, then a very young, inexperienced and naive solicitor, curious about the instructions he had received from his client, decided to ring the local social service department to find out 'what was known' about the family. He was naive in thinking that he could elicit information about his client or the family in the first place, but was even more surprised that a social worker would willingly divulge so much information over the phone. Even had the social worker known the person on the other end of the phone was who he claimed to be, and that he had accurately represented the reason for his inquiry, the social worker probably had no authority to release agency information in the way she did. Assuming Mrs Davis and/or her sons were clients of the agency, the social worker certainly breached confidentiality.

Case study 2

Greg is a counsellor for adolescents at a local youth refuge. He has been working with Tim, a 14-year-old boy who has left home. The refuge is a halfway house for boys who have been institutionalised for violent crimes, although others also stay there on an emergency basis. The current group of boys have been living there for several months and have formed close friendships with each other and the staff. Greg has promised that what Tim tells him will be confidential while they discuss issues of his past behaviour, including whatever happened between him and his parents and his previous history of drug abuse.

During one session, Tim reveals some information about a break-and-enter during which a man died.

'I'm glad I can talk to you about this, man,' says Tim. 'You see, Alex got the blame but he was only driving the car. He's too scared to talk because John and Bill will kill him if he tells. We were all there. Johnny hit the man while he was asleep. We only meant for him to stay asleep—we didn't know we killed him. Since Alex was the one driving and his prints were on the car, we decided to let him take the blame. All of us can cover for each other. Trouble is, he's the only one who hasn't done time. I hate to think what will happen to him in gaol—he's on remand now and it's already doing his head in. Don't tell anyone, man. Johnny and Bill will know who talked and I'll be dead meat for sure. They also know where my sister lives.'

'Don't worry, Tim. I keep my promises—your secret is safe with me,' says Greg, while thinking, 'It looks like it's one life against several, my own included.'

Case study 3

Fred and Ann have been married for a number of years and are now considering starting a family. Fred recently went to his family doctor for an examination as he has noticed a discharge and a rash on his penis. He tells the doctor that during a business trip to Sydney he had unprotected sex with a prostitute. Tests reveal that he has gonorrhoea and chlamydia. While both are treatable, the GP advises Fred to either abstain from intercourse for the time being or at least to use a condom. The GP cautions Fred that if he infects his wife this could have serious consequences for any future pregnancy.

Fred points out that they don't usually use condoms because his wife uses the contraceptive pill and, in any event, they are trying for a baby and his wife would become suspicious. Fred asks the doctor to say nothing to his wife.

Case studies 2 and 3 are variations of a common practice problem— that of acquiring information about clients or others that could create ethical dilemmas involving the scope and extent of the duty of confidentiality and how the duty can conflict with other responsibilities the worker might have—in these cases duties to protect or promote the interests of others. The other issue of concern is the professionals in each case making promises about the information that they have obtained without at least some reflection on what they ought to do. If Ann in Case 3 is also a patient of the doctor, the doctor has allowed himself to be placed in an intolerable situation. He may be forced to lie to Ann to keep his promise to Fred.

> **Case study 4**
> A school health team requests information about the Turkle family from the child and family health social worker, Heather, who operates from the same community health centre but in a different team. Heather has been providing family therapy to the Turkles for some months. The school health team has been asked to investigate the home situation of Billy Turkle, due to behavioural problems at school.

The final case study in this cluster represents a wider problem that professionals have with intra- and inter-agency relationships between professionals—the circumstances when information about a client can or should be shared with other professionals and agencies.

So, what might be the scope of a professional's obligations in relation to confidentiality and what is its relationship to privacy?

Privacy and social work

In the scenario in our last chapter, the privacy of the self-neglecting elderly woman was raised by two social workers as a possible defence to their failure to respond to the call for assistance. In chapter 2, Cara seems to have made an error of professional judgement in so readily bowing to pressure from the police and, in so doing, breached her client's confidentiality. Some basic knowledge of police powers and the circumstances under which she could be compelled to breach confidentiality might have helped her. More importantly, some understanding of her professional ethical duties in relation to client confidentiality, including an understanding of its limits or scope, would have been useful. In this chapter we pursue both the issue of privacy and its related concept confidentiality a bit further.

Privacy is defined as having both a descriptive (a factual, 'what is' description) and a normative ('what ought to be') dimension. This means that privacy consists of a descriptive condition, of someone not being interfered with and then having some ability to exclude others, while it is also held to be a moral right to be 'left alone'. Confidentiality is defined as the social worker's obligation not to disclose client information that is gained in the course of a professional social work relationship. Under the principle of confidentiality, personal or other information that is gained in the context of such a relationship cannot be used in a different context or for a different purpose by the social worker, unless legally permitted, or required, to do so.

The social work profession has traditionally regarded client confidentiality as a robust principle which, while not absolute, should not be easily overridden. Indeed, for social work students, it is one of the first ethical principles to which they are introduced when they begin their studies. While any profession, including social work, is free to choose the ethical rules and principles it wishes to prioritise as more important than others, it is nevertheless incumbent on it to justify why it should regard confidentiality as a first order or basic principle; a principle that is not derived from other more basic principles.

We hold the position that confidentiality is, in fact, a second-order ethical principle, or one that is used as a means to meet one of the fundamental ethical principles, for example respect for privacy or self-determination. Failing to acknowledge this leaves social workers open to dilemmas about confidentiality that have no basis for resolution. Moreover, social workers will lose sight of the relationship between confidentiality and respect for privacy.

As part of our discussion in this chapter, we are going to argue a number of things:

- that privacy is a neglected concept in human service work compared to confidentiality, even though codes of ethics may pay lip service to both principles;
- that social workers sometimes confuse or conflate the notions of confidentiality and privacy;
- that social workers tend to elevate the concept of confidentiality to the status of a first-order ethical principle; and
- that social workers sometimes fail to understand the scope of their ethical responsibilities in relation to confidentiality.

This can lead to irresolvable ethical dilemmas: whose confidentiality to protect? What to do when others' rights are at risk? How to ensure the best possible referrals and advice?

Privacy, confidentiality and professional codes

All professional codes have something to say about confidentiality. Some, like the Canadian code (CASW 1996), retain the traditional way of treating confidentiality as a primary principle in its own right. 'Confidential Information' is listed as the fifth of the 'Ethical Duties and Obligations' in the Canadian code, and it is the most detailed of all the chapters in the code. Privacy is not mentioned. Others, like the British (BASW 2002), North American (NASW 1999) and Australian (AASW 2000) codes, talk about privacy and confidentiality together and list them not as principles, but as part of ethical practice or practice standards. Just how the social work profession conceives confidentiality and privacy in any of these countries is therefore not an easy question to address.

The AASW code, for example, contains standards in relation to clients. Headed 'Information Privacy/Confidentiality', the first statement of this practice standard states:

> Social workers respect the right of clients to a relationship of trust, to privacy and confidentiality, and to responsible use of information obtained in the course of professional service (AASW 2000).

It thus implies that it is concerned with two separate but related principles: privacy and confidentiality. However, the seven clauses that follow this one are about the disclosure or non-disclosure of client information. The more general notion of privacy is not discussed. Similarly, while confidentiality is defined in some detail in the glossary, privacy is not mentioned. In the 'Guidelines for Ethical Decision-Making' confidentiality is discussed in some detail while a passing reference is made to privacy legislation. It is also interesting to note that when privacy is mentioned, it is only information privacy rather than any broader concept of privacy.

Similarly, the British code contains the heading 'Privacy, confidentiality and records', with the first clause stating that social workers will:

> respect service users' rights to a relationship of trust, to privacy, reliability and confidentiality and to the responsible use of information obtained from or about them (BASW 2002).

The NASW code states:

> Social workers should respect clients' right to privacy. Social workers should not solicit private information from clients unless it is essential to providing services or conducting social work evaluation or research. Once private information is shared, standards of confidentiality apply (NASW 1999).

Like the Australian code, these are the only references to privacy in the codes. The IFSW *Ethics in Social Work, Statement of Principles* includes a general guideline for professional conduct in relation to confidentiality that does not mention privacy at all:

> Social workers should maintain confidentiality regarding information about people who use their services. Exceptions to this may only be justified on the basis of a greater ethical requirement (such as the preservation of life) (IFSW 2004).

The argument that social work codes of ethics ignore the protection of personal privacy could be countered perhaps by arguing that the central commitment of the human services generally, and the social work profession in particular, to the principle of self-determination is, by implication, an acknowledgment of a person's privacy. Doing so, however, is to conflate principles that are not the same. Privacy is not a subset of self-determination, although the two notions are connected. For one thing, privacy is a necessary condition for the development of self-determination. Self-determination involves reflection and reflection requires a degree of privacy. For another thing, in order to exercise privacy rights a person may need to be self-determining, for example, choosing to refuse to become a client.

It may seem a bit absurd to talk of self-determination in a practice context where privacy has already been invaded and the person might have no choice about whether or not to be a client. However, if self-determination is seen as being a condition within which there is a continuum, this apparent contradiction is addressed. The 2000 Australian code goes some way in attempting to address these difficulties by stipulating that, especially when working with involuntary clients or in statutory contexts, social workers must be explicit about the limits of client self-determination, the limits of their own authority, and the options clients have in these circumstances but, while the invasion of privacy is perhaps assumed in such situations, it is not discussed. The confusion resulting from the implicit conflation of privacy and self-determination means that different practice strategies for protecting privacy, as against self-determination, are not recognised let alone made explicit.

We will take up the issue of privacy and its relationship to confidentiality in greater detail later on. Suffice it to say here that, while there is considerable confusion in relation to the distinction between these two notions in professional codes, in practice it is confidentiality that the profession is most concerned to protect. That is, it is non-disclosure in respect of the relationship between the social worker and client, as opposed to the privacy rights of the client, that is the particular concern of the profession.

Confidentiality

Finn (1992) has observed that in most professions, including the human services, the notion of professional confidentiality implies four propositions:

- information is not limited to that actually communicated by the client to the professional—it can include opinion derived from observation as well as the exercise of professional judgement;
- the duration of the obligation extends beyond the period when a person has ceased to be a client;
- the obligation can be overridden in some circumstances by other ethical considerations;
- the obligation is subject to compliance with the law, at least when the specific law in question is ethically defensible.

The third proposition entails the non-absolute nature of confidentiality. The principle of confidentiality can be overridden under certain circumstances by other moral considerations, including ones enshrined in the law. These would include the rights of third parties at risk from clients, and here we take it that any legal requirement is fundamentally based on moral obligations. The non-absolute nature of confidentiality is acknowledged in the Australian Association of Social Workers 2000 code, which obliges the social worker to 'inform clients fully about the limits of confidentiality in any given situation'. Nevertheless, there are problems with the idea of fully informing clients about the limits of confidentiality, and we will return to this later.

It is important to understand that confidentiality as the human service professions conceive it ought not to be taken simply as a matter of the right of a client. The first proposition above, for example, seems to imply that confidentiality extends beyond what may transpire between client and social worker so that, for instance, a social worker's opinions about a client may also need to be protected from disclosure. Additionally, the second and third propositions seem to imply that the existence of confidential information concerning a client, whether known to that client or not, may not be subject to any control by that client. Thus, when considering the principle of confidentiality in relation to information or opinion concerning a client, we need to ask whether it is client/social worker confidentiality or social worker/social worker confidentiality or social worker/employer confidentiality or social worker/third party confidentiality that is at issue.

The 'robust' principle

We suggested earlier that the social work profession has always tended to treat confidentiality as a robust principle and, all other things being equal, so it should. However, an Australian example typifies the problem of determining the basis of the principle of confidentiality. In that case, reported in the *Canberra Times* on 17 February 1995, the Australian Capital Territory (ACT) Administrative Appeals Tribunal allowed the name of an informant to the Woden Valley Child at Risk Committee to be released to the alleged perpetrator under the *Freedom of Information Act*—an allegation of sexual assault had been made against the grandfather of a child at the centre of a custody case. The head of the social work department told the Tribunal that the release of the informant's name to a third party was contrary to the AASW Code of Ethics and would lower the professional standing of the department. The head seemed to believe that these were adequate arguments against disclosure. Furthermore, it also seems the head believed that confidentiality was a basic principle and not one derived from more fundamental principles, in this case the right of individuals not to be exposed to untested hearsay obtained from a source the Tribunal said was potentially biased.

Compare this with another case in 1995 also involving an ACT social worker who was gaoled by a New South Wales magistrate, albeit for a few hours, for refusing to hand over counselling notes subpoenaed by defence lawyers in a rape case. At that time (the law was subsequently amended), the practice of subpoenaing counsellor notes was commonplace, 'not because lawyers truly believed there would be evidence in the notes to assist their client's case, but as "fishing expeditions" to see what might turn up. This social worker risked her own freedom to protect her client's confidentiality because she was worried that the private thoughts of rape victims communicated to their counsellors, which sometimes expressed their feelings of 'guilt' or 'fault', could be used out of context by unscrupulous lawyers (Cossins and Pilkington 1996).

It is no coincidence that the word 'confidentiality' derives from the Latin *fidere*—to trust—because one argument that is commonly used to justify the principle of confidentiality as a fundamental principle is the so-called 'trust argument'. Many professionals—doctors, social workers, psychologists—use the trust argument to treat confidentiality as though it is a robust principle. The argument goes thus: trust is necessary for effective practice, and confidentiality is necessary for trust, therefore confidentiality is a basic and robust ethical principle in practice. However, there is scant conclusive empirical evidence for the claim that a robust principle of confidentiality is necessary for trust and hence for effective practice.

Marcia Neave, writing about HIV and confidentiality, observed that:

> Unfortunately there is little empirical evidence bearing upon this difficult policy question. The extent to which preservation of

doctor-patient confidence affects willingness of individuals to seek medical help or to provide information about their sexual behaviour to their doctors is not really known. Findings about the psychotherapist-patient relationship (such as frankness of patients during interviews) have also been inconclusive (Neave 1987: 4).

Privacy in human service work

We have argued that the social work profession has paid insufficient attention to ideas about privacy in its accounts of what constitutes ethical practice. Indeed, we suggest that this failure leads to a distortion in how social workers understand and apply other connected central principles, such as self-determination and confidentiality. We suggest that the trust argument, for example, fails to sufficiently take into account the right to privacy that clients have in relation to information concerning their health, psychological wellbeing and intimate activities. Such privacy rights—rights that exist prior to the establishment of any relationship between client and worker—are at least part of the underpinning for the principle of confidentiality. A worker ought not disclose the psychological condition of his/her client because the client has a right to privacy in respect of such information, and the social worker is privy to the information only on the general (but defeasible) condition that he or she not disclose it to any third party. Respect for the right to privacy is in part derived from the more general principle of respect for people. Having an intrinsic respect for people consists in part in respecting their right to privacy.

We began this chapter with the thought that the notion of privacy has both a descriptive and a normative dimension. On the one hand privacy consists of being in some condition of not being interfered with or having some power to exclude and, on the other, privacy is held to be a moral right, or at least an important good. Most accounts of privacy acknowledge this much.

There are five aspects of the normative dimension of privacy—that dimension which tells us what privacy ought to be. The first two aspects are about personal information and the right to not be observed by others. The range of matters regarded as private usually includes things that could be referred to as a person's 'inner self'. We would regard it as unacceptable if someone demanded to know all about another person's thoughts, beliefs, emotions and bodily sensations and states. It may be thought from this that privacy and secrecy are related concepts. Bok (1984) defines secrecy as intentional concealment whereas, according to Fried (1968), privacy is concerned with the control individuals have over information about themselves as well as the ability to modulate the quality of the knowledge.

The third aspect of privacy is that it is a desirable condition or power or moral right about the interference in one person's life by the other person(s). (This is also taken to include occupancy of 'private space' by unwanted physical intrusions.) In particular, a person's intimate personal relations with other people are regarded as private. So while a lover, friend or close relation might be entitled to know certain things or to intervene in a person's life, others would not be so entitled.

Fourth, there are certain facts regarded as private by virtue of the impact of their disclosure on a person's various public roles and practices (Benn 1988). These kinds of facts are apparently regarded as private in part by virtue of the potential, should they be disclosed, of undermining the capacity of the person to function in these public roles or to fairly compete in these practices. If others know a person's criminal record, this may undermine their job prospects. If business competitors have access to my business plans they will gain an unfair advantage over me. If a would-be employer knows my sexual preferences he or she may unfairly discriminate against me.

Fifth and last, Westin (1967) suggests that privacy is 'an instrument for achieving individual goals of self-realisation'. Thus, a measure of privacy is necessary simply in order for a person to pursue his or her projects, whatever those projects might be. For one thing, reflection is necessary for planning, and reflection requires privacy. For another, knowledge of someone else's plans could enable those plans to be thwarted. Self-determination requires a measure of privacy.

Given this account of privacy, what can we say of the relationship of privacy to confidentiality with special reference to social workers? There are at least two kinds of cases in which confidentiality derives from the right to privacy.

First, there are circumstances under which a professional's knowledge concerning a client's inner self or intimate relations are in the client's interest. A doctor needs to know about a patient's bodily sensations and states, in so far as this is necessary for successful treatment and the patient has consented to be treated—similarly for psychologists and social workers. This 'need to know' for the benefit of the client gives rise to the principle of confidentiality. Such information, while available to the doctor or social worker, should still be unavailable to others, and for the doctor or social worker to disclose this information would constitute a breach of confidentiality.

Second, there are apparently circumstances under which a social worker may legitimately interfere in the life of a client, notwithstanding the fact that it is not in the client's interest or the fact that the client has not given his or her consent. Such cases include ones in which the client is harming, or is likely to harm, some third party, and cases in which the client is harming or is likely to harm him/herself and is not able to give informed consent. In these cases the professional has in fact invaded the privacy of the client, albeit possibly legitimately. It must be said that the existence of these cases in which the right to privacy is in fact invaded tends to be glossed over. This is hardly surprising given that to acknowledge a person's right of privacy may, after all, undermine the licence social workers have to involve themselves in the lives of others.

A further point here is that the right to privacy of the client may have certain consequences in relation to information gleaned in the course of what is in fact an invasion of privacy. In particular there is the consequence that as far as possible the invasion of privacy be contained. But such containment amounts to a requirement of confidentiality.

In other words, there is a duty to maintain confidentiality in respect of information obtained in the course of this invasion of privacy. But consider the problem that occurs in relation to familial genetic diseases, where screening or testing reveals that other family members are carriers or recipients of a genetic disorder. In this sense, it may be true that there is no such thing as genetic privacy in a family context because the testing of one person must invade the privacy of another. It nevertheless raises troubling questions about the value of the professional client confidential relationship.

Some practice considerations

Notwithstanding the assertions made by professionals about the importance of confidentiality, and regardless of what the client may think will happen to the information they might have imparted wittingly or willingly to the social worker, the idea that there is a confidential relationship between the client and the professional is often wide of the mark. Because social workers usually work in organisational environments, and sometimes even within some kind of legal or statutory framework, it is probably more accurate to understand confidentiality as a relationship between client and organisation. The social worker is the mediator between client and organisation and, to a degree, can regulate the quality and quantity of information about the client in virtue of the fact that they are compiling the client's case notes. However, the extent to which the client understands that their information can, and in all probability will, be seen by any number of other workers, including workers from other agencies and services, is doubtful. In many cases, codes of practice exhort social workers to explain the limits of confidentiality and, in some cases, agency policy might require clients to sign consent forms agreeing to the release of information.

Nevertheless, even with these limited safeguards, the concept of the robust principle is undermined. Social workers within the health care system have, in recent years, witnessed the problem of maintaining confidentiality because of the widespread introduction of centralised, electronic record systems. While there might be very good reasons for this trend, the primary one being the best interests of the patient, it does give rise to particular ethical concerns because there exists the potential for information to become less secure and more accessible. More importantly, even though all professionals within that health setting might be charged with similar obligations with respect to confidentiality, the real problem is the protection of the patient's or client's right to privacy. Social work case notes, for example, compiled by a hospital social worker working with the victim of sexual assault might contain intimate details necessary for the social worker to work with her client, but irrelevant to the nurse, pharmacist or even the doctor who could have access to the same client's records. System safeguards to prevent unauthorised access, even by other professionals, tends to undermine some of the very purposes for setting up centralised record systems in the first place.

There are other very practical problems associated with keeping client information confidential. Practitioners in rural areas face particular and peculiar difficulties their urban colleagues do not. They may be the sole worker in the agency. Faced with difficult cases and lacking collegial support and supervision, they may seek out workers in other agencies to debrief and share concerns. Unlike social services in urban areas, where caseloads can be shared by a number of workers, in a rural community the single worker will carry all the caseload of the community. Almost inevitably, when working with one client they will come across information about another, perhaps from the same family. Is it ethical to use that information, or should the worker adopt a kind of professional blindness? In rural communities privacy is also much harder to maintain and protect. The paradox of living more isolated lives is that one often becomes more visible to the rest of the community. Home visits by workers are noticed and become the source of community curiosity, speculation and gossip.

All social work interventions involve some degree of interference with an individual's privacy. Before social workers can maintain confidentiality they must gain information about someone or something and this must, by definition, involve infringing a person's privacy, even if it is with the person's consent (in itself a problematic concept). Because of their licence to intervene in the lives of people, social work duties with respect to privacy and confidentiality extend beyond those who are their immediate clients to those who are not yet their clients, or who may never become their clients.

Virtues

The virtue appropriate to the principle of confidentiality is discretion. Discretion is a very traditional virtue that straddles a fine line between morality and etiquette. In the context of vocational ethics, the use of the virtue of discretion is helpful in understanding the complexities of confidentiality as a principle that we have discussed in this chapter. Discretion is not the same as secretiveness. Instead, the discrete person is one who will not share information about others for trivial or self-seeking reasons. The discrete person doesn't gossip. The discrete person is also honest with those who share personal information. They would not let someone share a confidence in the mistaken belief that this information would be kept secret, then discuss these secrets behind the confidant's back. Instead, it seems necessary that discretion demands a frank explanation of whom the information may be shared with and a justification of this sharing in terms of the confidant's best interests. This said, discretion doesn't typically mean that confidences won't be shared. Within suitably intimate relationships, such as marriages, partners would be reasonably expected to share things they know without any requirement of disclosure. Such intimate sharing is just what people should reasonably expect, at least in regards to confidences of a personal nature.

The discrete social worker would be someone who does not discuss confidences without good reason, and who is frank with clients about how information may be used. Discretion does not rule out reasonable sharing of information among groups of colleagues who have reason to know and a role in the client's relationship with an agency. Discretion requires ethical practitioners to treat information as valuable and precious, and to act always from the perspective that knowledge of others is a trust to be treated with respect. In this way the virtue of discretion is a useful concept to make clear the relationship between the values of autonomy and respect for persons, the principle of confidentiality and the potential moral value of simple social etiquette, observance of which is a way of expressing our respect for others. In this regard reflection on the virtue of discretion also reminds us that clients are entitled, at the very least, to the same expressions of social respect that others would expect.

Ethical skills

The discussion of confidentiality in this chapter highlights the central role of collaboration or team work in skilful social work. This is a good example of the many ways in which what might be thought of as simply technical social work skills in fact rest upon, and give effect to, ethical principles. A social work student who accepts the central role of ethics in the profession will do well to pay extra attention to classes that teach the practical skills of team work, and will also do well to develop those skills we associate with the term 'bureaucratic competence', especially a sound understanding of how various roles, professions and management functions interact in an agency. The ability to collaborate is of particular importance in setting limits to the circulation of information, and in deciding just where information should circulate.

Ethical knowledge

The discussion of confidentiality draws attention to the complicated role played by ideas of rights in social work practice. We have discussed rights in the first part of this book. In the next chapter we will discuss rights theory in greater detail in the context of tolerance and diversity. Before we look at rights theory it will be useful to look at the complexity of the application of the idea of a right in a practical context like confidentiality. If we accept that clients have a right to confidentiality, then the discussion in this chapter makes clear that this right is quite complex. Mainstream rights discourse can often suggest that rights are absolutes. A right is often asserted as if this will end an ethical argument. Ronald Dworkin has described rights as 'trumps', considerations that override any of the other perspectives we have argued carry equal weight in ethical reasoning (1977: 153). However Dworkin's position is not as absolute as it may sound, since he is merely arguing that social policy should never treat individuals or minorities as dispensable in search of overall utilitarian outcomes. His argument is focused on the demand that government should protect the interests of all citizens equally. This does not mean that the assertion of an individual right should override any other principle, goal or interest. Instead a claimed right may be over-ridden or defeated by other ethically weighty considerations, giving rise to the idea that rights are defeasible. This means that if we identify a right we must still proceed with an argument that will identify any other rights, interests, consequences or obligations that might weaken or nullify the right. Not all rights may be defeasible. Some who regard life itself as sacred might regard the right to life as absolute (but not all such people by any means). Nevertheless it certainly makes sense to view the right to confidentiality as a defeasible right, a presumption in favour of privacy that can be overridden for certain reasons.

Conclusion

Both privacy and confidentiality are important professional principles for social workers but they are neither absolute nor inviolate. How the principles are worked through and applied in practice is very much context bound, and practitioners must always be mindful how their professional application undermines or promotes the interests and well-being of clients and others. Social workers have to accept they do not live in a perfect professional ethical world where all principles operate in harmony.

Study tasks

1   What does your code of ethics have to say about privacy and confidentiality? To what extent are the statements about confidentiality qualified?

2   If you have had some experience working in a social service, think about how matters involving client confidentiality were handled. Was there any agency policy covering client information, collection or dissemination? Were there any procedures to deal with inter-agency relations?

3   Professionals are entitled to private lives. If you were in the situation of Mike and Jane (case study 1), what would you do? Would you have handled things differently?

4   In many jurisdictions social workers that work with children are legally required to report children they consider to be at risk of harm. Consider how that duty might conflict with your ethical duty to maintain confidentiality and how that duty to report impacts on the social worker-client relationship.

5   In case study 2 do you think Greg is ethically obliged to honour his personal promise of secrecy to Tim? Why? How do you think Greg should have handled the situation? Do you see any differences between a personal promise of secrecy and professional confidentiality?

Further reading

Bok, S. 1984, *Secrets: On the ethics of concealment and revelation*, Oxford University Press, New York. Along with Wilson (below) a classic on privacy and confidentiality.

Etzioni, A. 1999, *The Limits of Privacy*, Basic Books, New York. Offers a populist account from a communitarian perspective on privacy in the United States.

Wilson, S. 1978, *Confidentiality in Social Work*, Free Press, New York.

Websites

Office of the Federal Privacy Commissioner (Australia) <http://www.privacy.gov.au/>.

Office of the Privacy Commissioner (New Zealand) <http://www.privacy.org.nz/>.

European Data Protection Supervisor, responsible for monitoring the processing of personal data by the European Community institutions and bodies <http://www.edps.eu.int/>.

Privacy Info <http://www.privacyinfo.ca/>. A site maintained by Professor Michael Geist of the University of Ottawa, Faculty of Law. The site features links to Canadian privacy legislation, privacy law news, and other resources.

8
Social control and toleration

A young pregnant woman talks to Karen Brown, a counsellor in a community health centre about her support needs. During the interview she discloses that she was subjected to FGM as a child in her country of origin. Karen knows that FGM (female genital mutilation), also known as excision or female circumcision, is practised in Africa, the Middle East and parts of Asia. FGM generally involves the excision of all or part of the labia and even the clitoris. The procedure is usually carried out by elders or midwives and it is often done with broken glass or the lids of tin cans. FGM is illegal in all western countries but it has proven very difficult to eradicate, despite the efforts of community activists, social workers and legislators.

To Karen's surprise the young woman tells her she will seek to have her child 'circumcised', because a girl 'cannot be offered for marriage if she is not clean'. The woman is aware that the practice is illegal, and that no medical practitioner will perform it, but she knows of 'backyard' operators in her community who will do it.

It is important to bear in mind that throughout the world FGM is being opposed not just by western liberals, but by activists and community groups within the cultures where it is practised. It would be simplistic to characterise the debate over FGM as one between cultures, as it is actually a struggle going on within various cultures struggling with issues of identity and power.

If you were Karen, how would you have responded to this disclosure? Would you have tried to dissuade the young woman? Would you have alerted child protection authorities? Would you have tried to have her child taken into care? Should she have been threatened with jail if she proceeds?

We would imagine that a case like this would challenge you, not just because the practice of FGM will offend against many values, but also because it is not at all clear if a practice a client regards as essential to her identity should be coercively suppressed by someone from a radically different culture. The case is also complicated by the recognition that coercion may be unnecessary and even ineffective. Should others in the client's community who are working to change attitudes be sought? Should the client be assisted in order to minimise possibly unavoidable harm to the child? Should cultural practices that your society does not approve of be respected?

In this chapter we are looking at the related problems of tolerance and social control. They are related because, in some ways, they are two sides of the one coin. To the extent that your society does not tolerate certain practices, collectively your society is inclined to try to control them, and to compel or convince people to live in ways more compatible with the morals and culture of your society. Your reaction to the hypothetical case described above will be conditioned by the dynamic of control and tolerance. We can predict one of two broad responses. Perhaps you are conflicted by experiencing both.

On the one hand there is the typical relativistic response, something like 'Who am I to tell other people how to live?' Many social work students experience this kind of reaction to problems created by cultural diversity. They link the truth of moral claims, such as 'FGM is bad', to culture, and claim to believe that what is right for us is not necessarily right for others. Philosophers call this 'cultural relativism', the idea that moral beliefs are derived directly from cultural norms and are not subject to any rational critique from outside that culture.

The alternative response is one we might dub 'absolutism', the idea that all moral judgements are rational and universal. The absolutist is inclined to judge people harshly for gross deviations from apparently universal moral standards. Since FGM seems to violate a number of basic precepts, such as respect for autonomy (see chapters 6 and 7), beneficence (the injunction to do good) and non-maleficence (the injunction to do no harm), the absolutist would think the client should be subject to coercion and punishment. Her liability comes from the absolutist's belief that she 'ought' to be able to see that it is wrong.

It is our intention to steer clear of both of these extremes by exploring how to best balance respect for diversity with the obligation to act on our sincere moral and ethical beliefs.

Social control

'Social control' is a term derived from critical social work literature, where it usually refers to the tendency of social workers to impose a middle-class or mainstream morality and lifestyle on clients. In the process they use power granted by society to force marginalised and 'deviant' clients to conform. The power that social workers deploy is both legal and economic. In some situations workers can mobilise the power of courts and other enforcement agencies, coercing clients who fear imprisonment or the risk of losing their children for non-compliance with court orders. At other times workers can control access to resources that clients desperately need. In both sorts of situations the worker enforces rules concerning access to services and standards of satisfactory compliance which are, in turn, derived from dominant social norms concerning work, patterns of residence, behaviour, family structure, hygiene, economic obligation and deference to authority.

There is a clear link between the tendency for social workers to act as agents of social control and moral absolutism. This absolutism is often bolstered by the worker's social position. Educated, middle-class people typically receive a great deal of positive reinforcement and are embedded in the dominant class and culture of their society. As a result they have a lot of faith in their own judgements and can easily see their own way of life as 'natural' and 'appropriate'. To the extent that social work has been a vocation of the middle class, social workers have been liable to see their role in absolutist terms. This can lead to domineering and coercive practices. In dealing with people from marginalised cultures, members of poorer classes, and those with 'deviant' moralities or lifestyles, social workers can mistake their emotional reactions for firm moral truths.

For example, in the grim past of the profession, social workers in many countries were involved in various child removal practices. In the colonial New World, children were often removed from indigenous families on the excuse of neglect, when in fact social workers were actually complicit in policies of assimilation. These policies are now widely denounced and may even fall under the UN's definition of genocide (*Convention on the Prevention and Punishment of the Crime of Genocide*, Article 2). In England and other industrialised countries, single mothers were coerced into signing away their parental rights and had their children removed straight after birth. Some were even told their children had died. This was done because the middle class shared a consensus that single mothers were unfit parents simply because of their supposed moral lapses. The policy also spared the state the expense of providing income support to single parents. These various child-removal policies are all cases of social workers acting as agents for the imposition of a dominant and oppressive ideology on the powerless.

To the extent that social work is part of social movements and organisations indigenous to the community this dynamic of control is far less likely.

Relativism

The relativist's response is often welcomed by those who want to resist the tendency to social control. This is because relativism forces workers to consider the basis of a client's beliefs and behaviours and to treat these alternative cultural perspectives with respect. There are a number of arguments in favour of the relativistic stance. The most obvious is simply that it is clear that not all values upon which people act and which define our ideas of a good life belong in the rational, interpersonal space of ethical discourse. There are many things that influence your moral or evaluative position, such as religious and metaphysical beliefs, and insights derived from experience and emotion which are important but which you could not, and probably should not have to, defend.

In addition, you might note that terms such as 'better' and 'good' are not fixed. They are relative to some point of reference or referent. As Aristotle (2002: 10–13) observed, something is good only relative to its purpose or function. A good wine must have flavour and bouquet; a good axe must have a sharp edge and be well balanced. So a good family will be one that meets each of our own ideals of what a family is for or what it should do. A good life is one that meets our idea of what people are for, or our ideas about human nature. We all must be careful how we use evaluative terms like 'good', because we can easily imagine that we are using terms of universal validity when we are actually presupposing our own values.

However, just because we don't want to see some of the worst examples of social work's collusion with 'cultural' and other forms of imperialism repeated is not an argument for adopting the opposite pole of relativism. It is apparently quite natural for humans to think in terms of simple oppositions; 'black and white', 'north and south', 'good and bad', 'male and female' are all examples of simple oppositions or contrasts that are both obvious and misleading. Just as the distinction between male and female can blind us to the diversity and complexity of human biology and sexuality, the conflict between absolutism and relativism can obscure alternative ethical positions that occupy the middle ground between them.

James Rachels (2003) has argued, very convincingly, that relativism is fundamentally self-contradictory and tends to violate many of society's basic moral intuitions. 'Culture' is far too indefinite and complex to be a firm truth-maker for moral claims. The reliance on culture ignores moral minorities within cultures, and also those whose backgrounds are multicultural. Relativism might prevent each of us from imposing our values on others, but it also stops us from intervening in even the greatest evils. There are some things we each have good reason to think are wrong regardless of context, things which no culture ought to accept, such as torture and genocide. The grounds for judging these to be evil seem to be universal ones and susceptible to rational justification.

Perhaps Rachels' (2003) most telling argument against relativism is that it can create obvious absurdities. If culture is the basis for morality, then the majority beliefs of a culture must be true simply because the majority believe them. If a majority view weren't sufficient, then the relativist would have to believe that any culture lacking complete moral consensus has no true moral beliefs at all. So the relativist seems to be committed to the view that the majority of members of the dominant Anglo–American culture were correct in their belief that the chattel slavery of black Africans was morally acceptable, and that the Quakers and other opponents were wrong. That is, until the opposition succeeded in winning a majority to their views, when the anti-slavery view became true and the previously true pro-slavery view became false. This implication that moral judgements are subject to a kind of majority vote is just patently absurd and would seem to invalidate cultural relativism (Rachels 2003: 21–3).

The lessons of relativism

Having dismissed relativism as a viable alternative to traditional moral absolutism or universalism, Rachels sounds a note of caution. He refers to the 'lessons of relativism', and we will follow him in suggesting that it would be hasty to imagine that the failure of relativism gives any comfort to the absolutist. He argues that the insights that motivated the relativist retain their validity. It is essential that we take care to avoid haste in reaching our judgements, and are especially careful to ensure that we filter out emotional responses, prejudices and assumptions when we consider moral questions. Each of us should be careful to note the effect of culture, class and religion on our judgements. These factors don't necessarily have to be eliminated. A significant part of all personal values are derived from these sources. However, as we discussed earlier in this book, the action-guiding function of ethics draws on a wider set of reasons than the evaluative and deeply personal realm of morality.

As a profession social workers should be careful that the policies they support and the actions they perform do not rely on reasons that people from different backgrounds cannot also respect, especially if they are going to be affected by those actions. Social workers must always bear in mind that their professional actions must be able to be justified or explained to other stakeholders. The final challenge of relativism is to think carefully about what can be reasonably said to those who might object to what we do (Rachels 2003: 29–31).

Perhaps the most fruitful outcome of Rachels' discussion of relativism is his focus on context. Rachels argues that the diversity of views and practices we observe can be explained by what we have called the values–principles distinction. He claims that while practices vary widely, many of them are actually derived from the same set of basic, universal values. One example he uses is the practice of infanticide. Many cultures, including the industrialised West, deplore infanticide as an obvious and repulsive wrong. However, other cultures have practised it. But, if we look carefully at the contexts of this practice it is clear that infanticide only occurs in marginal environments where the survival of the family is at stake, places such as in the Australian and African deserts and the Arctic Circle. Once people had access to secure food and water supplies, modern medicines and other goods, the practice was abandoned.

Rachels believes that these differences in practices can be explained by the need to apply the value of caring for children in a harsh environment. He claims that all humans share the belief that as parents we have an obligation to do what is best for our children. However, if a shortage of food will cause a child to starve slowly to death and perhaps kill the parents too, then the kindest thing to do may be to kill the child quickly.

It is not an easy choice, but it may be the right one in the context. It emerges as a sort of rule, excusing infanticide under defined conditions, but the rule or principle is derived from the very same value that supports our general repugnance for infanticide. Examples like this lead Rachels to the conclusion that humans actually share a pretty stable set of basic values, but that the variety of conditions under which people live causes these values to be applied in very different ways. If we understand the context it is possible to come to an understanding of, and even endorse, the principles others live by (Rachels 2003: 23–9).

This leaves a significant challenge. If we are going to avoid the evils of controlling or imperialist (absolutist) practice without surrendering our moral judgement to relativism, we are going to need some way of drawing a line. This is where the ethical concept of toleration comes in.

Diversity and toleration

The idea of toleration has its origins in the English Reformation, when members of minority dissenting sects argued for equal rights of worship and conscience. This struggle for religious equality laid the basis for the doctrine we now know as liberalism (introduced in chapter 3), the idea that individuals are entitled to live according to their own values and idea of a good life. The only constraint that liberals respect is the rule that each person is not entitled to do what they want if doing so will restrict the equal rights of others or cause them some other kind of harm.

In chapter 3 we discussed John Stuart Mill, the founding father of liberalism. Mill's most influential argument was that liberty is essential to human welfare because the free development of the personality is crucial to each of us fulfilling our potential and living a life that is good for us (1987: 118–41). This idea is the origin of the modern value of autonomy, which we discussed in chapter 6. In the context of toleration this liberal value is deployed to provide the basis for principles of practice that define the proper boundary for our own moral judgements.

.ındary has several elements. The most important element
ɔ the boundary between morals and ethics. Morals are deeply
ɹ and have to do with each person's judgements about good and
baᴄ ɹs observed, they cannot always be subject to criticism by others.
Ethics on the other hand are action guiding and have to do with how,
as professionals, we relate to others. This distinction allows each of us to
avoid the relativist mistake of abandoning our own moral judgements.
Instead, we need to recognise that our individual moral beliefs ought not
to be the sole basis for action. Since moral judgements have multiple
sources beyond the reach of straightforward rational debate, it is appropriate that we defer to a client's moral choices when those choices affect
their own lives. We sometimes call this 'epistemic modesty', in other
words, acknowledging you don't know everything. This just means that
we each ought to be careful not to impose our own judgements on others
as if we had better grounds for our values than other people do.

Obviously, as in confidentiality conflicts, this deference stops when
people's choices harm others or are grossly illegal. The move from the
evaluative sphere of morality to the action-centred sphere of ethics also
involves recognition of extra, non-evaluative reasons. These can also stop
each of us imposing our values on others. The major form of such
reasons is consequentialist (see chapter 3). Sometimes, perhaps often, the
attempt to force people to do what they do not believe they ought to do
can cause harm to them and those around them. These are among the
harms that Mill first envisioned in his liberalism. The kinds of harms
that can result include disengagement from services, acting out, resent-
ment, mistrust of authority, and the factionalising of welfare provision
along religious and other lines, reflecting a breakdown of the bonds of
civil society.

A secondary element of the boundary enclosing our own moral
judgements lies in respect for the value of autonomy. If you believe, as
early liberals like Mill and Emmanuel Kant did, that respecting an individual's capacity for choice is essential to respecting their unique moral
worth, then you will refrain from imposing your own judgement upon
them, even when you have good reason to believe that their choice is

wrong or even harmful. This is a matter of ranking values, so that we can decide which value might be more compelling when they conflict. If autonomy and self-determination rank highly as values then they might often outweigh other values and even some consequences you regard as bad.

Interestingly, the order may not be the same in every situation. This means that it isn't set. In one situation you might decide that autonomy is more important than beneficence, but reverse this order in another context. There is probably no value so absolute that it always outranks every other value. However, higher ranking values are so important that they will normally retain their importance and only be knocked off under unusual circumstances. This is why we can rely upon rules of thumb. One crucial rule will be that respect for the autonomy of others should outweigh your moral evaluation of their actions. Clearly, this is a rule of thumb and it will be defeated by any actions that cause serious harm. In very extreme cases your own moral judgement about what is harmful may override a client's values. Our point is not that you should never act on your own moral judgement, only that great care must be taken in overriding someone else's beliefs, and that such impositions must be treated as exceptions and as last resorts requiring considerable justification.

A third element of the boundary is derived from Rachels' idea that universal human values get their apparent diversity from the contexts in which they are applied. We sometimes call this 'context-dependency'. It is perhaps the clearest example of how moral judgements are only a part of the ethical decision-making process. Sometimes when we want to get someone else to do what we think is right we say, 'If I were you, I would . . .' However, if you were me, perhaps you would do exactly what I do. Before you decide whether or not to intervene in someone's choices, you should check to ensure that the context of choice facing that person is not so different that you would revise your own opinions in a similar situation. There can often be unseen or misunderstood factors at work, which is why you should exercise caution in overriding a client's judgement. These considerations lead back to the rule of thumb supported by autonomy, but add an extra condition: our deference to the client's judgement will also be overridden if their context contains no conditions that would alter our judgement. There is a limit to the ways that the context can distort basic values.

While Rachels can rely upon some sound empirical evidence for his argument that humans share basic values, the nature of these values remains somewhat mysterious. The Nobel Laureate Amartya Sen (1985: 9–16) has developed what he calls the capabilities approach, based on the idea that all people need capacities, like literacy or mobility, in order to live whatever life they desire. The American philosopher and jurist John Rawls (1971: 62) used a similar theory, basing our social and civil rights on a basket of basic goods every person needs in order to live their version of the good life. Rawls' list includes nutrition, health, shelter and self-respect.

The philosopher Joseph Raz (1986: 165–92) described how fundamental needs, which are universal to all humans, connect to rights only when there is some group or some person who can meet the subject's fundamental need or interest by way of some specific act. The act will depend on the current situation, including the society's level of economic development, technological sophistication and so on. For example, every person has a basic need for food. A person has an interest in securing a food supply, and so may fix an interest in the available local food supply. However she only has a right to that food if there is some barrier to her getting it; perhaps it is all grown on private land. Her right to access that food gets its original moral force from her morally important need for food. This becomes a right only if there is a barrier preventing her from meeting her own needs and some other person, the landowner perhaps, who has the capacity to meet that need.

On Raz's account, rights come and go and are dependent on the context, and the existence of someone who bears the corresponding obligation. So, in our previous example, the right being claimed might disappear if there were not enough food to go around (although a desperate conflict may break out instead). The nature of the right might change if the landowners were poor, but the government was in a position to buy surplus food from them and give it to the starving. This argument explains how we each can have universal basic needs or interests, but context-dependent as well as culturally relative rights and obligations.

This family of theories allows each of us to understand how the great variety of human beliefs and values can arise from a universal base. To the extent that practices are reasonable responses to the challenge of meeting basic needs, each of us has no cause for worry when others live differently to us. To the extent that value conflicts arise from rational responses to divergent circumstances, we should be cautious about crossing the cultural divide without understanding other people's circumstances. However, if a belief or practice clearly damages the interests of stakeholders even within their own context, then as social workers we have a basis for rationally justifying intervention.

Toleration does not encompass only cases where it is clear that people are reacting to different circumstances. It also includes cases, such as the original religious examples, where it is not possible for anybody to say that another person has made an obvious mistake. While the truth of your own religious beliefs may be obvious to you, it is not clear that everyone has equal access to that truth, that the truth is exclusive, or that other people could easily apprehend what you know unless they had your experiences. Some basic metaphysical and moral beliefs just don't admit of rational criticism or empirical inquiry, so the principle of toleration is often extended to cases where we shouldn't criticise others for holding views we think mistaken, and should not expect to be able to make them change their mind.

As a result there are three quite separate arguments for toleration that might apply in different circustances: the argument from consequences (forcing people to change their ways may do more harm than good); the argument from context; and the argument from what we have previously called 'epistemic modesty'. We might also call it the argument from uncertainty.

The limits of toleration

All of this leads to the resolution of the basic question: when is it permissible to substitute our own professional judgement for that of a client? You already have most of the resources to answer this question, because it is closely related to the resolution of the paternalism conundrum from chapter 6. However, toleration is somewhat different because in this instance the client is not incapacitated, more that they are simply wrong. What is needed is a rule of thumb that will allow you to decide when disagreement should be resolved in your favour.

Gross illegality and harm to third parties are typically overriding in cases of value or judgement substitution. The challenge is that there is no agreement among reasonable people about what constitutes 'harm'. In the case of the young woman who is sincere in her belief that circumcising her daughter will be to the child's benefit, preventing the procedure in the eyes of the mother would harm the child because she would be unable to marry within her community. The closest you can get to a resolution would be to rely upon the basic needs approach described above. If you seek to prevent the woman performing FGM, you would argue that her child will lack certain capacities or will have her self-esteem undermined by it. Or you could argue that she will be unable to access some ideals of a good life foreclosed by having the procedure. The severe damage to her health caused by the procedure, accompanied by pain and the risk of death, would probably be sufficient since good health and the right to life are pretty fundamental.

Arguments justifying intervention can follow two broad lines. First, you can argue that a particular belief or practice is wrong. This is a potent claim, for it involves the conviction that in its own context the belief or practice never served the basic interests of those affected by it. This is a very hard claim to sustain, and it will often fail because it is impossible to show that one's own response to a situation is uniquely true. The extreme case of FGM, and other cases such as human sacrifice, will be among those that probably succeed. The second, more common line is to argue that changing circumstances have altered the context, so much so that a practice that was once quite just is no longer justified. The various cases of infanticide we canvassed earlier fall into this category.

Virtues

Tolerance is a virtue. It is normally defined as a willingness to allow or to not interfere with things we think are wrong. It should not be confused with valuing diversity. Positive acceptance of difference is obviously also a virtue but it isn't tolerance. Be very careful not to confuse these two. People can easily think that their obligations to diversity end as soon as they feel confronted, threatened or offended. The virtue of tolerance requires a capacity to endure these and other negative emotions when reason tells us interference is not justified or will make things worse.

In order to foster a suitable tolerance the worker needs to work hard on the practice of epistemic humility. A critical attitude, a degree of detachment from one's own values, and an even temperament are all required. The best practice is always to step back from any judgement in order to interrogate it from the other person's point of view. This is harder than it sounds because we don't have the time to sit and reflect on every choice we make. One's peers can be helpful in setting the general framework for good practice and can act as a sounding board in hard cases. If in doubt, talk it out.

In the case of the young pregnant woman that began this chapter, toleration will involve a careful assessment of the harm caused if the baby undergoes FGM, versus the harm done if you intervene. It is in this sense a utilitarian ethical judgement, albeit one motivated by clear values. We have already argued that FGM is indefensible generally, so the question becomes one of strategy. Practicalities such as finding out the levels of support and opposition to FGM within the woman's own community, here in the country to which she has emigrated, will help. Depending on the situation, some discussion of the differences in context and changing practices, particularly if held with an influential community member, may be all that is needed. Sometimes reminders of the penalties for breaking the law, including the law on child abuse, will help someone realise that they are now in a new system with new rules and ethical practices. It may seem contradictory to be discussing imposing one's values like this as an example of toleration. The point is, if this discussion comes from a place of tolerance within the worker, there is more likely to be genuine respect and understanding for the client's desire to do the right thing for their child, which in turn will build a bridge of trust and openness through which both sides can reassess their positions and feel more free to change their minds.

Tolerance does not necessarily mean always refusing to become involved. It does mean that one is careful to act only from reasons that the other party can accept, even if they don't agree with the conclusions.

Ethical skills

This discussion of tolerance might suggest a focus on not acting, and yet in reality it brings us back to the central tenets of ethical social work practice. The real lesson of the discussion of tolerance is to remind us to break a dangerous dichotomy between doing nothing and imposing one's own views through the techniques of social control. Ethical activism is the name we give to the bundle of social work skills involved in community development and individual empowerment. In the FGM example with which we began this chapter, it is likely to be far more fruitful to engage the young woman's community, especially other women who are striving to break out of traditional roles. The social worker will do well to support and resource groups working from within that community rather than to impose their own vision of how this woman ought to live. It is worth remembering that there may still be need for tolerance. A community that is developing according to its own values may still not adopt all the attitudes of the worker. Instead, we must ask if the solutions adopted by that community meet the needs of its members. The solutions may not be ones we would choose for ourselves, but that doesn't make them wrong.

Ethical knowledge

The term cultural relativism is a good one to fix in your vocabulary, but it is quite complex. All forms of relativism share the idea that the truth of a belief is not fixed, it changes depending on circumstances. This is a difficult concept to get clear, because we are used to the idea that truth is absolute. Many beliefs are of course, no relativist denies that. However, different kinds of relativism believe that statements about beliefs change their value depending on who makes those statements and under what conditions. Some ethicists, called emotivists, have held that a statement of the form 'that is wrong' depend for their truth on the emotional reaction of the individual. If I react badly to seeing someone kick a dog I may say 'kicking dogs is wrong' and this will be true for me. If you don't react the same way the same statement may be false if you say it. Cultural relativism is the belief that one's cultural context makes moral claims true or false, so that if my culture regards dogs as almost persons, then kicking dogs is wrong for me. If your culture treats dogs as unclean then kicking dogs may be okay for you. As the discussion above will have suggested we do not regard cultural relativism as a sound theory because of the difficulty in deciding just what a culture as a whole believes.

Conclusion

It is a commonplace now, almost a platitude, that diversity is valued. For example, it is the second element of the IFSW's (2004) explanation of social justice. The problem is nobody seems quite sure exactly why diversity is so valuable. We won't try to answer that challenge here. The question might be usefully debated in a classroom or seminar setting, but don't expect any firm results. Our preference is to demystify the diversity issue by focusing on the persons and communities that contribute to this diversity. Each is valuable in its own right. People simply matter. We take this moral intuition to be incontestable. Access to goods and opportunities in order to live a life that is meaningful and valuable is high in social work's ranking of values. The communities that people live within also matter, at the very least because each community provides the framework for a form of life essential to the self-conception and self-expression of those who live in it.

The actual value of diversity may be obscure, but we have more than enough pragmatic and moral reasons to be extremely cautious about imposing alien ways of life on people. As Mill observed, even if we are certain that our own beliefs are uniquely true and our way of life is best, we will still harm people by forcing them to conform. A way of life would have to be extremely bad to outweigh the harm we would do by stamping it out. The loss of the language, rituals and art forms which we use to express our unique world view leaves us mute and rudderless. This is the fate that has befallen many indigenous communities, and the harm continues for centuries.

Nevertheless, there are times when social workers must intervene. The substitution of one's own value for those of a client is an occasion for extreme caution, but it will be justified where the harm the client's actions cause outweighs the harm they will suffer if we impose our values. If those harmed do not share the client's values then subjecting stakeholders to these actions in simply unjust. Otherwise an intervention will be justified where a context has changed or an action violates such basic interests that it is never justified in any context.

Study tasks

1   Thinking about the case study and the cultural differences involved, imagine what it must be like for visitors from other countries to watch some of the things we do. Pick on one practice, ritual or other highly structured behaviour you are involved in, or something you do as part of your family or community. It might be attending or participating in a sporting contest, a religious celebration, a festival, a wedding, religious inductions for children such as a birth or christening, a public

holiday. Write a brief description (perhaps one page) of this event or practice from the point of view of an alien observer who can see what is going on, but does not know why it is occurring or the significance of this activity is.

2 Now, on another page attempt to explain from your own (informed) perspective just what is happening and why in order to help this outsider better understand and perhaps appreciate the significance of, and why you are participating in, this activity.

It is naturally very difficult to adopt someone else's standpoint. However, these exercises should help you suspend your usual acceptance of your own way of life and perhaps see how some things you take for granted may seem strange and even wrong or foolish to others. In writing your reply to the outsider you should focus on the beliefs and meanings that underpin your practices, and try to explain what it is about them that makes your actions right, meaningful, good or fun. Bear in mind that the outsider is not going to be moved by answers such as 'it's just tradition' or 'we've always done it that way'. This is an exercise in cross-cultural communication, so you'll need to find ways of explaining things that hook into things other people also understand and respect.

Further reading

Aristotle 2002, *Nicomachean Ethics*, translated and edited by Christopher Rowe, Oxford University Press, Oxford. While reading a complete work of philosophy, especially classical philosophy, is something of a challenge, this work is remarkable for its clarity. Readers will particularly benefit from an awareness of the substantive arguments in favour of virtue ethics. While there are many more modern approaches to virtue ethics, Aristotle's version is explicitly teleological and so much closer to the approach we use in this book.

Herodotus 2003, *The Histories*, translated by Aubrey de Selincourt, edited by John Marincola, Penguin, Harmondsworth. This work is a classic in its own right, but is of special interest because of the interesting conflicts between moral viewpoints that seem alien to modern eyes. Herodotus is also the original source for the idea of cultural relativism.

Mill, J.S. (1859) 1987, *On Liberty*, Penguin, Harmondsworth. Mill's argument for individual rights and diversity is the basis for a lot of modern rights discourse. It is especially interesting because of the way in which he blends utilitarian, deontological and virtue-based arguments in support of a rights framework that is usually thought to be purely deontological.

Rachels, J. 2003, *The Elements of Moral Philosophy* (4th edn), McGraw-Hill, New York. This is a standard introductory text that will be very helpful for readers seeking a better understanding of the strengths, weaknesses and uses of various modes of ethical reasoning. His argument against relativism is the standard in philosophy, and his discussion of the lessons of relativism is the basis for much of the argument in this chapter.

Rawls, J. 1971, *A Theory of Justice*, Belknap Press, Massachusetts. This work is the inspiration of a lot of modern work in distributional justice (one of the bases of social justice). Rawls' list of basic goods is particularly influential.

Raz, J. 1986, *The Morality of Freedom*, Clarendon, Oxford. Readers are particularly encouraged to read the sections on the nature of rights, which are the basis for the link between interests and rights which is one of the sources of the pluralistic method in this book, particularly because it links rights with consequences in a way that makes rights discourse a lot less mysterious.

Sen, A. 1985, *Commodities and Capabilities*, Elsevier, Amsterdam. Sen's work on capabilities is an excellent source for basic goods or common human needs. His arguments concerning the link between democracy and economic development are very useful for discussions of social justice.

Sidanius, J. and Pratto, F. 1999, *Social Dominance: An intergroup theory of social hierarchy and oppression*, Cambridge University Press, Cambridge. A good introduction to the theory of social control and the ways in which it is achieved. Chapter 4, on consensual ideologies, is especially useful for social work settings.

Websites

Amnesty International <http://www.amnesty.org/ailib/intcam/femgen/fgm1.htm/>. A useful starting point for readers wishing to know more about the practice of FGM and the strategies employed by its opponents.

Internet Encyclopedia of Philosophy <http://www.iep.utm.edu/t/tolerati.htm/>. The entry on Toleration (the act) as opposed to tolerance (the virtue) is good as it includes a section on epistemic toleration, which relates to the idea of epistemic humility.

Part four
Ethics—the source
of power in
social work

9
Ethical decision-making

It is the year 2020. Gina and Harry (from chapter 3) are both senior social workers in the global organisation People Management Corporation. They are still friends and continue to meet for coffee occasionally. These days, both are on time. Today is Friday and Harry is waiting for Gina, who has been to an ethical decision-making workshop. Gina arrives, sits down in the booth, and takes out a small black plastic card.

'Our problems are solved,' she announces. 'Here it is—the new EDM card, with extra features tailored to your company, your position, and your risk rating.' She presses her thumb to one corner. 'Confidentiality is assured too. Once my thumbprint has initialised this baby, it won't talk to anyone else. From my thumbprint it knows where I work, my position and all the other variables it will need to make the right decision for me. It fits in my wallet. Anywhere and any time, no matter the situation, the players or even the country, I just put in the question, and out pops the answer. No more dilemmas, no more debates. And I can use it as evidence in a court of law if necessary. As long as I follow the card's advice (and it keeps a record of what it has said), then there's no argument about what I have done. It's guaranteed foolproof and has one hundred per cent accuracy. Takes the risk out of all kinds of people work.'

'Wow,' is all Harry can say. 'What if I don't like what it advises?'
'Advises?' retorts Gina. 'Who cares if you know you will be
doing the right thing all the time? This little card takes the worry out
of work. It balances everything up—the needs and rights of the
various stakeholders, the outcomes at the end of the day, the principles along the way, the cultural factors, laws and, of course, your
own levels of risk in the situation. Harry, we'll be so efficient now,
the place of all helping professionals in the People Management
Corporation will be assured.' She carefully places the card back
into her wallet and pats the wallet into her small black wireless
organiser.

'Oh and did I mention? It's an organiser as well—upgrades your
present system with links to home and office too. My problems with
my teenage kids are over.'

This chapter draws together the three themes developed in previous
chapters—ethical virtues, skills and knowledge—to make explicit
our approach to ethical decision-making. We argue that the good social
worker is able to combine moral judgement with dispositions developed
through a process of critical reflection. Practice which is ethically
grounded in this way provides a professional stance that is more active,
effective, inclusive and empowering, i.e. ethical practice. We begin by
examining some of the more formulaic approaches to ethical decision-
making models.

Sometimes the dream of an EDM card (as in the case study above)
is very tempting. At times social workers, who are mired in the swamp
of reality and caught between unsavoury choices, would love to be able
to pose their dilemma and have it answered immediately. And not only
social workers. Recently there has been an explosion of ethical decision-
making models in business, psychology and other professions (Cottone
and Claus 2000; Robertson and Crittendon 2003). There are also several
good critiques of these models. However, unlike other professions, social
work is wary of advocating for specific ethical decision-making models.

By this stage you too should be wary of uncritically accepting the idea of a single, formulaic approach to ethical decision-making. Nonetheless, there have been many recent attempts to create this very thing. This chapter begins with a review of the different types of ethical decision-making models available, mostly of those in counselling roles, and considers their usefulness for social workers and social work students in the field. We ask, what role do ethical decision-making models have for practitioners interested in ethical practice?

What are ethical decision-making models?

Ethical decision-making models are systematic ways of thinking through ethical dilemmas. Usually they are a series of steps or questions that you answer in sequence to work your way through to a solution. With the huge number of ethical decision-making models available, there are now several different ways of classifying them. Three useful reviews of ethical decision-making models are those by Cottone and Claus (2000), Garcia et al. (2003) and Minor and Petocz (2003). Each of these papers has a slightly different way of classifying ethical decision-making models, and all make important points that practitioners should understand. Although they draw somewhat different conclusions about what is needed to make these models work, together they form a helpful basis from which to examine them.

The three types of ethical inquiry that we highlighted in chapter 3 all make different contributions to ethical decision-making and ethical decision-making models. First, it is important to understand and be explicit about the meta-ethical assumptions that underlie the particular ethical model. We need to know how right and wrong are understood and defined. Minor and Petocz (2003) argue that it is only when we are clear about this that it is possible to have a coherent model. For example, does the model have a naturalistic view of right and wrong or a non-naturalistic one (based on a concept of God's law for example)? Next, we need to be clear about whether the ethical decision-making model is trying to describe/explain how people behave (descriptive ethics), or whether it is attempting to tell people what to do (normative or prescriptive ethics). These distinctions were discussed in chapter 3, when we defined the ethical territory in which we would be working. Minor and Petocz (2003) discuss the trouble that ethical decision-making models get into when they slide between describing and prescribing—they point out that often models that claim to be describing ethical behaviour actually end up trying to tell us what to do.

Most prescriptive ethical decision-making models are based on one or more of the ethical approaches that we cover in this book (consequentialism, deontology, normative relativism and virtue theory). One point of agreement among the reviews of these models is that despite all the arguments for and against each approach, none of these approaches is sufficient, on its own, for effective ethical decision-making.

Minor and Petocz (2003) make three important criticisms of current ethical decision-making models. First, the models fail to adequately distinguish between prescriptive (what we should be doing) and descriptive (what people are actually doing) models. Second, the models fail to explicitly acknowledge their underlying assumptions. Third, they are not comprehensive enough. Minor and Petocz claim that these three criticisms apply whether ethical decision-making models are implicit or explicit about the theories upon which they are based, and whether only one, or more than one, moral theory is involved.

We now examine some of these models in more detail.

Rational model

This type of model, also known as a cognitive model, relies on a rational decision-making process to sort out which course of action to take once conflicting moral principles have been identified. Usually there are several linear steps set down for the professional to take. Garcia et al. (2003) cite Forester-Miller and Davis's (1995) seven-step model as an example:

(a) identify the problem, (b) refer to the code of ethics and professional guidelines, (c) determine the nature and dimensions of the dilemma, (d) generate potential courses of action, (e) consider the potential consequences of all options and then choose a course of action, (f) evaluate the course of action, and (g) implement the course of action. (Garcia et al. 2003: 3)

Other rational models have different numbers of steps, for example Welfel's nine-step model (cited in Garcia et al. 2003). Minor and Petocz (2003) make the point that difficulties arise when prescriptive ethical decision-making models incorporate professional codes (as in the one cited above). They argue that the more practice is guided by prescriptive and explicit codes, the more it becomes a general, cognitive decision-making model and the less room there is for personal values or philosophies. These authors also show that there are different ways in which codes are used, citing Koehn (1994) and Coady and Bloch (1996), both of whom justify the use of codes for different reasons, and neither of whom, Minor and Petocz argue, ground their justification in moral theory. Minor and Petocz (2003) claim that when professional codes are incorporated into decision processes as norms, they risk ending up within a framework of normative relativism and therefore lose the ability to guide professionals in what to do. In other words, if the procedure tells you to do whatever your code happens to say then judgement about what to do gives way to the spurious idea that whatever a code happens to say is true, just because it is your code. Worse, if your code collects together a set of values and principles that can themselves conflict, and which are expressed only in general terms, then it will not provide the definite prescriptions that the model claims it will.

Virtue ethics models

There are quite a few versions of ethical decision-making models based on virtue ethics, one of the normative approaches to ethics that we identified in chapter 3 and on which we rely for our approach to ethical practice. Instead of judging moral rightness on the act or decision itself, as one does in the rational model, in a virtue ethics model moral rightness depends on the personal qualities of the practitioner. In Jordan and Meara's model these qualities include integrity, prudence, discretion, perseverance, courage, benevolence, humility and hope (cited in Garcia et al. 2003; Minor and Petocz 2003).

Some of the problems associated with this and later models based on virtue ethics is that it seems impossible to judge how to act based on the qualities of the practitioner alone. Also, there is no one list of virtues—Garcia et al. (2003) cite Freeman's (2000) and Tarvydas's (1998) virtue-based models, each containing different lists of essential virtues.

Prescriptive models that combine theories

Both Minor and Petocz (2003) and Cottone and Claus (2000) examine a range of models that try to incorporate several ethical theories, for example, outcomes, duties and virtues, and sometimes rational decision-making steps and personal values and attitudes as well. Cottone and Claus (2000) review a large number of 'how to' ethical decision-making models for counsellors. They conclude with surprise that most of these models pay little attention to their philosophical foundations and are not at all clear about their theoretical assumptions. They point out the lack of research into whether these models work, and highlight the lack of understanding about what makes a good ethical decision-making model. These authors tentatively suggest that some blend of the virtue-based approach with different ethical principles (such as utilitarian thinking and duties/rights-based theories) may be the way forward. For example, Tarvydas's (1998) integrative decision-making model combines an analysis of the ethical principles underlying competing courses of action, along with the morals, beliefs and experiences of the individuals involved. Cottone (2001) went on to develop the social constructivist model, which is based on the assumption that ethical decision-making is primarily a social or interactional phenomenon. This model incorporates psychological and sociological theories.

Minor and Petocz (2003) argue that it should be possible to develop prescriptive models of ethical decision-making that combine different ethical approaches, as long as they include rational or cognitive components, are clear about their underlying meta-ethical assumptions and provide detailed consideration of situations where rights and consequences conflict. They cite Swanton (2001) and Hursthouse (1999) as authors whose virtue-based models come close to meeting these criteria. Such authors begin with explicit meta-ethical assumptions (for example, naturalism), develop a general account of a desirable state of affairs (such as a just and caring society), consider the foundational principles contributing to this desired outcome (in the case of social work, these would be human dignity and human rights, and social justice) and then specify the virtuous motivations required to promote such a state of affairs (competence, integrity, compassion etc.). In each situation, according to Minor and Petocz, the person would be required to justify the particular virtues, duties and outcomes they choose.

We find it particularly interesting that so many of the more recent ethical decision-making models advocate a plurality of perspectives. Despite their lack of attention to their theoretical base, it seems that these applied models by practice-focused writers are in tune with some of the most recent theorists now writing about professional ethics. Perhaps experience of real life and complex practice problems brings the realisation that good ethical decision-making needs to encompass many perspectives, just as more theoretically oriented writers are realising that principles previously seen as being irreconcilable may actually be complementary and related.

The transcultural integrative model

Respect for cultural diversity is one of the five elements of social justice discussed in chapter 4, so important for all social workers. In chapter 8 we discussed the difference between respecting diversity and toleration. In their review of ethical decision-making models, Garcia et al. (2003) review five different models of ethical decision-making for counsellors, finding that while multicultural concepts are being used in counselling models, they have not found their way into ethical decision-making models. These authors then propose a 'transcultural integrative' model of their own, which they feel synthesises the strengths of the other models and also takes into account cultural differences between the various players involved in ethical problems and dilemmas.

To each of the four stages of Tarvydas's (1998) integrative model, Garcia et al. (2003) add transcultural dimensions. Also incorporated are aspects of Cottone's (2001) social constructivist model (in particular his strategies for negotiating, consensualising and arbitrating between different parties when agreement is not possible) and Davis's (1997) collaborative model (which adds group discussion and collaboration to ethical decision-making). Together, this creates an ethical decision-making model for counsellors which Garcia et al. claim is able to include and respect cultural diversity.

This model is particularly interesting because it incorporates many of the ingredients that we argue are needed for our approach to ethical practice. First, the model involves a list of virtues needed by counsellors for ethical decision-making. These include reflection, attention to context, balance and collaboration (from Tarvydas's 1998 model) to which Garcia et al. add tolerance, sensitivity and openness. Next, the model requires consideration of a number of ethical principles.

Step 1 involves interpreting the situation through awareness and fact finding, with a particular emphasis on sensitivity to all the parties' cultural identities, acculturations and role socialisation, including those of the worker and any intragroup differences that might affect the ethical decision-making process. Step 2, 'formulating an ethical decision', is similar to the rational model outlined by Forester-Miller and Davis (1995), with additional cultural elements built into each of the steps in the model. This means that the worker reviews all the cultural perspectives, including potentially discriminatory laws and regulations, at each stage, consults cultural experts if necessary, and tries to reach agreement with all parties involved. Garcia et al. (2003) claim that the different ethical approaches, including virtue ethics, are reflected in steps 1 and 2, with their emphasis on counsellor sensitivity and awareness and using a rationale for reaching a final course of action.

Step 3 involves 'weighing competing non-moral values and affirming the course of action'. This may sound a little contradictory (how can one have 'non-moral values'?) but actually means reflecting on your own personal blind spots and any contextual and/or cultural issues that might influence the values you select and decisions you make. It would also involve legal constraints, organisational costs, practical limitations and other practical issues. Finally, step 4 involves planning, implementing and evaluating the course of action, including anticipating any contextual and cultural barriers that may interfere with the decision or course of action.

If agreement cannot be reached about how to solve the ethical dilemma or problem in step 2, the three-stage interpersonal process described by Cottone (2001) is brought into play, culminating in the use of a consensually accepted arbitrator, if agreement cannot be reached through discussion and negotiation between the parties. Elements from Cottone's (2001) model and Davis's (1997) collaborative model are most in evidence in steps 2 and 4 of the transcultural integrative model, where collaboration is used to reach agreement and implement the final resolution.

From this brief account, it can be seen how this model of ethical decision-making involves many of the elements of ethical practice that we have discussed: a number of ethical approaches (virtue-based ethics and a range of ethical principles), as well as collaborative and collective approaches to solving ethical dilemmas. However, our approach to ethical practice is designed for a wider range of social change interventions than just counselling, and does not claim to be an ethical decision-making model. Rather it offers a framework through which individual practitioners can become ethically active, and an argument to re-position ethics as the central driving force of social work.

The inclusive model

A more recent approach to social work ethics is found in the work of Chenoweth and McAuliffe (2005: 88–98). Their approach, which they call the 'inclusive model' of ethical reasoning, avoids the problems of linearity and excessive complexity we have identified in the other models. Instead Chenoweth and McAuliffe use a simple circular model which emphasises the interrelatedness of various aspects of ethical reflection. At the centre of this model are four core aspects of ethical practice—accountability, consultation, cultural sensitivity and critical reflection—surrounded by a series of interconnected steps such as defining the problem, 'mapping legitimacy' (identifying stakeholders), and seeking out alternative solutions (see Figure 9.1). This model is a significant step forward in the development of reasoning models because it emphasises the importance of

Figure 9.1: An inclusive model of ethical decision-making

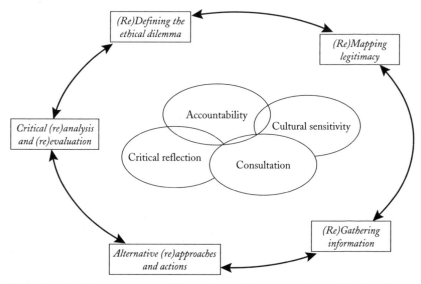

Reproduced with permission of the authors: Chenoweth, L. and McAuliffe, D. 2005, *The Road to Social Work and Human Service Practice*, Thomson, Victoria, p. 96.

personal responsibility while the circular structure reminds readers of the open-ended and interdependent nature of ethical argument.

While we believe the inclusive approach is an invaluable tool for mapping aspects of a specific moral problem, it shares the focus of other models on the resolution of dilemmas. It is certainly a superior approach to resolving specific practice problems, but we are also interested in explicitly connecting dilemmas to the wider domain of ethics that we have argued is the basis for good social work practice. The pluralistic approach we have adopted to formal ethical reasoning requires both a more explicit reliance on ethical theory, and that the decision-making process does not place the modes of analysis in opposition.

A 360-degree approach to ethical decision-making

We have argued throughout the book that while morality is about values and making judgements, ethics is about action. Even when we think something is right or wrong we still have to decide how to act. To act ethically requires us to balance our values, goals and responsibilities before we can make an all-things-considered decision.

Ethics is interpersonal and social—it is about how we treat each other and how we act in our world. In chapter 1 we considered how our postmodern world makes us more interdependent than ever. Therefore, ethics is about responsibility and interdependence. In chapter 2 we also discussed the dangers of ever-increasing regulations, and how sticking to formulas or specific codes of conduct is one way to avoid our responsibility to act ethically. There can be no simple formula by which we make ethical decisions. It is not a code of ethics that binds social work, but rather the shared understandings and commitments that underpin the code. Ethics moves beyond rules and relies on discretion.

In our postmodern, interdependent world, ethics is about relationships. Richard Hugman (2003) draws on the work of Bauman (1993) and ideas from feminist ethics of care (Sevenhuijsen 1998) to argue that ethics is about 'being-for-other', a relational exercise in which we each take responsibility for others regardless of whether the others deserve it or respond in kind. A corollary of this is that ethics is a major concern of every person—it can no longer be left to the experts. Hugman (2003: 11) writes: 'An ethics of care approach in social work would require that each practitioner be conscious of the integration of the moral dimension with the technical choices they make in their practice.'

Part of being interdependent and relational is the requirement to be inclusive. Good ethical judgements rely upon discussion and consultation, with our peers, our supervisors, our clients and in society generally. Some social work codes of ethics advocate consultation as part of ethical decision-making (for example the AASW 2000) as do some experienced social work ethics practitioners. Freud and Krug (2002), social workers with many years' experience on ethics committees in the United States, for instance, recommend that social work ethical dilemmas be solved in small group discussions so that a range of opinions and intuitions can be considered. Throughout this book we have stressed the importance of open discussion and a collective approach to resolving ethical dilemmas. In most situations, more heads are better than one.

Another key theme of this book and ethical decision-making is that ethics is plural. Ethical pluralism is about balancing various imperatives. Many ethical theorists, and some social work ethicists, still maintain that you have to choose 'one' or 'the other' approach to ethics. Traditionally, supporters of rules and obligations (followers of Kant or deontological approaches) oppose those who advocate that outcomes and goals such as social justice are most important (utilitarians) and the principles of each side have been seen as irreconcilable (see chapter 3). Within social work another example is supporters of virtue-based ethics, such as McBeath and Webb (2002), rejecting both duty-based ethics and utilitarian ethics as mirroring the current neo-liberal focus on process and outcomes in favour of virtue ethics, which emphasises the sort of person the social worker is.

Instead of having to choose one approach we, along with other social work theorists such as Richard Hugman (2003, 2005) and Sarah Banks

(2001), argue that there is something of value in every approach—that no single approach can represent the 'truth' about ethics. Just as our codes of ethics reflect a plurality of approaches, practical judgements require us to balance the three major modes of ethical thinking that we have been studying in this book:

- commitment to rules and duties, especially upholding human rights and human dignity;
- commitment to goals and outcomes, especially social justice;
- commitment to being a certain sort of person—practising the virtues of integrity, competence, compassion and so on.

Practical judgements also require us to maintain a critical attitude. This means including useful aspects of postmodernism, such as questioning the meanings of language and recognising the power that discourse has to structure our understanding and decisions. We need sociological, psychological, political science and philosophical knowledge to analyse the contexts in which we make our choices before we can make a proper decision about how to act.

Thus, ethical decisions depend on a 360-degree assessment. This involves the idea that we circle around, looking at each aspect or mode in turn, before we make our decision to act. We might start with our goals and then look at our rules to see if they match and then whether, in following our goals, we are being the kinds of people we want to be. Or we might turn the other way and start by critically examining our goals. You can't question everything at once or there is nowhere to start. Balance is what we are after, not a radical doubting of everything.

This heuristic imagining of a circle of reflection avoids the problems that beset most of the models we looked at in this chapter, which share a linear approach to problem solving that in turn suggests a mechanical resolution of complex problems. For example, we noted earlier that the introduction of codes of ethics as an early filter in a linear decision-making process would be problematic as it leads to relativism, and so disempowers the worker as a moral agent. However, earlier in this book we argued in favour of a more central role for codes in ethical practice.

If we think of the code not as a filter but as a sounding board or a source of ethical perspective, then it can still play its proper role. It cannot tell us what to do, but the code does act as a window into the on-going ethical debates of one's profession. The 360-degree assessment can include engagement with the code, and a comparison of the professional consensus it provides with our own values. This process casts a fresh light on both aspects of our decision, rather than promoting one as authoritative over the other as the linear models tend to do.

One of the key skills in engaging in a 360-degree assessment is, of course, critical reflection. This requires a high level of personal awareness so that we can recognise our own blocks and prejudices as we attempt to act ethically in the world. Also fundamental is the ability to critically analyse our environment and the political context that structures our decision. This is where the discursive and collaborative element of the better models becomes so important. The circle of reflection builds on the approach developed by Chenoweth and McAuliffe, but includes a role for the theoretical modes and the codes of ethics. It also emphasises the standards and principles that lie at the heart of good practice. This model is designed both as a device for addressing specific problems, and also a way to develop policies, rules and approaches to the many practical challenges that require adaptation and creativity.

One weakness of the transcultural model, inherited from its sources, is the insistence upon consensus and agreement. Ideally, colleagues should be able to work through a collaborative communication process to arrive at a shared decision that reflects everyone's perspectives, needs and concerns. However, this should not be built into a model by insisting on arbitration. Ultimately, the ethically responsible worker must decide for herself if she will endorse the decisions of her colleagues, bosses or employers. This is not the same as agreement of course. Sometimes, we go along with things because, all things considered, it is best to allow others to act on their own ethical beliefs rather than fracture the workplace by promoting disputes over relatively minor disagreements. This is an ethical decision in itself, and it allows the dissident worker to voice a contrary opinion at the appropriate times. In this way diversity is respected.

The circular process advocated by Chenoweth and McAuliffe and developed here also scores over the linear models in having no specific terminus. Lines have ends, circles don't. Workers live through and engage with an on-going ethical practice. Ethics and worklife are permanently fused. It is a mistake to think of ethical dilemmas as isolated events. They represent crises or peaks in the ethics process that require particular focus. The resolution of a dilemma or crisis, though, is not a return to an ethics-free normality, to 'business as usual'. Each crisis represents an opportunity to learn and to alter practice through reflection. Ethical challenges should be seen, not as crises to be overcome or averted, but as opportunities to improve the ethical framework within which all social work takes place. This direct challenge to the current management culture of crisis management and control is one of the major points in our approach to ethical practice.

A final advantage of the process we advocate is that it avoids the formal complexity of a decision-making model. As you may have noticed in reading the discussion of the models in this chapter, the allure of a model is that it will simplify hard ethical decisions by structuring them. Unfortunately, the simple models are riddled with flaws that make them unsuitable for the real world. Various authors have addressed these flaws, but in doing so they have created models that actually demand complex, multi-part processes that don't offer the clear structure and guided decision-making that was the whole attraction of a model to start with. Models of the sort developed by Garcia et al. (2003) do return to an appreciation of the complexity of real-world ethics, but they are so complex, open-textured, discursive and adaptive that they cease to function as effective models. It is better to give up on the goal of a decision-making model and focus instead on process.

Process-focused ethics is actually simpler in many ways because the practitioner is called upon to engage in discussion and debate, educate herself, and exercise some practical wisdom in knowing when the time has come to terminate debate by acting. It sets up the ideal of a practice environment characterised by discussion, openness, mutual respect and focus on the goals of one's profession. It does not require anyone to be expert in the application of highly complex and jargon-ridden formal procedures, of which there are too many in social work already.

Virtues

Philosophy derives its name from a compound of the ancient Greek words meaning the 'love of wisdom'. Wisdom is obviously an important character trait that can help people to be morally good, successful and happy. Wise people are also of great help as supporters and advisers. Clearly it is a virtue, a desirable capacity or character trait that contributes to moral conduct. The problem with wisdom is that it is very hard to define. Unlike courage, for example, we cannot give an easy formula for wisdom. Perhaps we might look back to Socrates, the father figure of western philosophy. When he was defending himself in court against charges of impiety and corrupting the youth of Athens, he claimed that he was wiser than other people only because, unlike them, he knew that he didn't know anything! It is perhaps more proper to say that Socrates' wisdom lay in not assuming authority to speak about things of which he was ignorant. The archetype of the know-all and the blowhard is as recognisable today as it was then (Tredennick 1969: 49–52). In this light wisdom might also be called good judgement, the very practical faculty of knowing when to judge, when to speak and when to reserve judgement and look for more information. Open-mindedness, practical wisdom, moral courage, reflectiveness, situational awareness, and sound research and analytic skills all contribute to good judgement. The ability to see all sides of a problem, especially through speaking with others, and to look at all parts of a problem are essential to good judgement. The common social work principle of non-judgementalism could be said to be an aspect of good judgement as we have defined it here. While non-judgementalism is normally presented as a rule it is really more like a virtue, because rules govern conduct not attitudes, but refusing to judge or being non-judgemental are attitudes.

Ethical skills

Knowing when to reserve judgement and when to terminate reflection and debate by acting is easier said than done. However, there are methods for arguing and analysing that will make it easier. Over time, practising the more formal methods of critical reasoning and ethical analysis is like practising any other difficult task. They begin as formal knowledge but with use become skills. Over time repetition makes them more like second nature, and they are transformed into virtues. One concept that can help to give more form to the idea of good judgement described above is the philosophical concept of scepticism, the idea that we might be mistaken about anything we believe and so should proceed very carefully, making sure that we have figured out what counts as proof or justification for any proposed belief before we assent to it. René Descartes, a great French thinker of the Enlightenment, proposed for argument's sake that we might be mistaken about our physical existence but not our existence as such, and from there built a system for verifying our beliefs that became the foundation of much western scientific method (2003: 72).[2] A more prosaic example would be the common problem of seeing a familiar face in a crowd. Often as not from a distance we will notice one or two features of a person that bring to mind someone we know, but this can be a mistake caused by the simple mechanics our minds use to retrieve memories. After a few embarrassing mistakes we learn to check our facts before we rely on the tricks memory can play.

Let's turn to the 360-degree assessment approach discussed earlier in this chapter. It relies on the sceptical methodology, and uses the ethical standard of justification to resolve our doubts. This means that there isn't a mechanical system for delivering a 'right' answer, but rather a standard of adequacy by which each person must judge for themselves

---

[2] The phrase 'I think therefore I am' is popularly attributed to Descartes, but it is a summary of his views which he never wrote, a bit like 'Play it again, Sam'! What he actually wrote was 'I am, I exist'.

Figure 9.2: An example of the circle of reflection

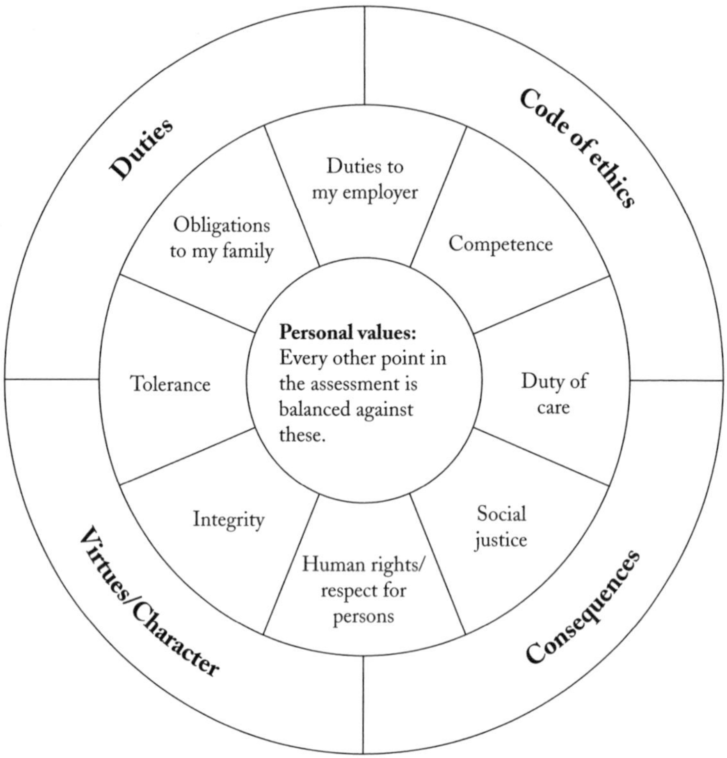

that they have good grounds for a decision. There is also no ultimate list of what should be on the 'wheel'. This is why we don't present the assessment as a decision procedure or model. It is just a heuristic device to help you in thinking about ethical problems. Nevertheless it may be useful to consider an example. The 360-degree assessment can be presented graphically as the circle of reflection, representing the various principles, virtues, goals, standards and ethical modes (Figure 9.2). One version could include 'duties to my employer', 'obligations to my family', 'social justice', 'tolerance', 'human rights and respect for persons' and 'integrity' (just for example).

This wheel is just an example. Each person's set of important points will vary, often including some aspects of ethical reasoning very generally (such as consequences in this list) but focusing on some detailed aspects (such as social justice in this list). Note also that some more common terms can replace technical ones (integrity is standing in for virtue in this list). The exact list depends on your own values, the professional values and goals you regard as most important, local differences in practice concepts and many other factors. The only definite advice we can give is to make sure that the three main modes of ethical analysis, obligation, virtue and consequences, and taking your own social work code of ethics into account all appear somewhere on the list at least once. In this version, the three modes are arrayed with the professional code around the outside of a ring of specific principles, modelling a relationship between general and specific standards and showing where some principles rely upon more than one value or ethical perspective. Ultimately the technique of circular reflection simply requires that all elements are consulted before a decision is reached.

Since people tend to emphasise one more than others you will probably find a bias creeping in where you use several items in your list that are all aspects of one mode. This is all right. Since we are imagining a circle it also doesn't matter where you start. All that matters is that you have considered all the relevant spokes at least once. Sometimes you will revisit a particular aspect in light of considerations arising elsewhere. Go round the wheel until you feel satisfied that you have resolved your doubts or, if the doubts or conflicts are irresolvable, that you know which consideration is decisive. The most important functions of the wheel are to slow judgement and ensure you have considered a range of possibilities before acting.

Ethical knowledge

Argument is one of the most important tools in the ethical practice toolkit. As you discuss and debate with colleagues new options become available, and fresh perspectives illuminate the problem. In previous chapters this knowledge theme has introduced some specific concepts that help make arguments more fruitful and reliable. When the 360-degree assessment approach is utilised as a part of the inter-personal ethical process a useful tool is a thought experiment, which also goes by the more technical name of a 'counterfactual'. Thought experiments are simple stories that you use to explore what you think would happen if the situation under consideration were changed slightly. Philosophers mostly use thought experiments to test intuitions and to sift out the most decisive principles from the complex of motives that we find in the real world. The stories used in thought experiments can be changed, one bit at a time, to see whether people will change their mind and thus to find out what specific aspect of the situation was really most important. In an ethical argument you can use these little stories to find out what modes of reasoning or what principles are really decisive. For example, the possible consequences of a situation might seem of overwhelming importance, but when you imagine the situation slightly changed so that the consequences change, you might discover that you would make the same decision anyway so that another aspect of the situation is actually what is determining the ethical judgement you make. Many of the case studies in this book, especially the made up ones (like the stories about Gina and Harry), are examples of thought experiments.

If the situation is unclear it can be very useful for a group to conduct some brief experiments. Look at each aspect of the problem and workshop some scenarios to see what emerges as the most important elements and then focus your thinking on these. The key to successful thought experiments is to keep the story simple, to change just one element at a time and see what if anything changes, and to keep things hypothetical. Don't use it as a way to attack people or to solicit disclosures from them, or else they won't collaborate properly and the results will be unreliable.

Conclusion

Ethics is a process, not a structured procedure that can be applied mechanically. Nevertheless there are processes and techniques you can apply. The 360-degree analysis will allow you to seek guidance from a comparison of many sources, and to seek alternative perspectives on your problems from your colleagues. It is important to critically compare the competing sources of judgement, including your own values and moral judgements, the professional consensus embodied in your code of ethics, and the experience of your colleagues and supervisors. However, the self-conscious engagement with this technique will occur only sporadically. It is essential that your practice in between crises promotes openness and communication so that you are constantly learning from and con-tributing to a reflective and collaborative practice.

Study task

Choose a case study, either from this book, from class or from real life. Subject it to a 360-degree analysis and decide what you would do, all things considered.

In conducting the analysis, try to draw up a 'wheel of reflection', placing on it those general and specific principles, modes of reasoning, and practice standards that seem to be involved. At the centre include any of your personal beliefs and moral commitments that might be at stake. Describe the process that brought you to your final judgement, noting if you actually went through all the parts of the circle. Describe how you balanced any competing commitments, and what factors caused some of these items to be discounted or over-ridden (if any). This description of your process prompted by the wheel will look a lot like an argument or justification.

If this is a class exercise you might consider analysing one case and reading out your analyses in class for debate.

Further reading

Alexandra, A., Matthews, S. and Miller, S. 2002, *Reasons, Values and Institutions*, Tertiary Press, Croydon. This textbook explains basic steps and tools in critical reasoning and informal logic, and links these to normative evaluations of various public institutions to show how reasoning about values can be applied.

Banks, S. 2001, *Ethics and Values in Social Work* (2nd Edn), Palgrave Macmillan, Basingstoke, Hampshire. Chapter 8, 'Ethical problems and dilemmas in practice', pp. 160–85 is an excellent chapter focusing on the skill of reflective practice in ethical decision-making, drawing out the issues through detailed case examples.

Cohen, S. 2004, *The Nature of Moral Reasoning*, Oxford University Press, South Melbourne. A handy, easy-to-use guide to the complexities of ethical decision-making. Tends to take a more complex view than we do, but it will introduce students to the wide variety of ways that moral theorists approach decision-making. Some good material on the uses and limits of models, chapters 12 and 13 are particularly relevant.

Hugman, R. 2003, 'Professional Ethics in Social Work: Living with the legacy', *Australian Social Work*, vol. 56, no. 1, pp. 5–15. A compulsory ethics article for all social workers—students and practitioners. Discusses the nature of social work ethics and how a range of perspectives, including utilitarian, Kantian, feminist ethics of care and postmodernism can be usefully employed.

Websites

Walter Maner from Boston University has constructed a chronological index of decision-making models <http://www.cs.bgsu.edu/maner/heuristics/toc.htm>. The index is intended for use by computer science students but includes a wide variety of models, showing the evolution of decision-making methodology. Some of the examples will be very useful in reflecting on the variety of ways models are used, and their limitations.

10
Ethics: The source of power in social work

This last chapter draws together the conclusions we have developed throughout the book about ethical social work practice. We will not revisit the arguments; rather we will summarise the key concepts and conclusions we have made.

Ethics involves practical decision-making and action. At its core ethics seeks to answer questions about how to contribute to the good life. Social work ethics is about how to be a good social worker, where 'good' means being the person who is best able to fulfil the purpose or 'telos' of social work (chapter 1). Ethics is an all-things-considered process, not a mechanical technique—it involves making a 360-degree assessment and relies upon the virtues, skills and knowledge of the practitioner, particularly their abilities to be reflective, self-aware and to consult.

Our approach to ethical social work practice offers an antidote to the defeatism, defensive practice, fragmentation and powerlessness that many social workers experience. It is about making change efforts from within organisations. It involves bounded ethical practice and satisficing, or the skills of making 'good enough' ethical decisions (chapter 2). Social workers working from this kind of ethical base are ethical activists, making their ethical voice heard wherever they are.

In chapter 2 we discussed Justin Oakley and Dean Cocking's (2001) definition of a profession as an occupation that serves a valuable social purpose and delivers goods that contribute to human flourishing. We agree that the most important elements of professionalism are adherence to a code of ethics or ethical standards, good judgement, client-centred practice, independence of thought or action, and competence (Oakley and Cocking 2001).

Ethical social work practice

Having considered in Part One three challenges to social work practice (the social-political context, the professional context and the nature of ethics itself), in Part Two we suggested ways that social work could meet these challenges. Our central argument is that social work needs to reclaim ethics as its heart and driving force; that we have to move ethics in from the margins and make sure that every social worker becomes ethically active. In our vision, with ethics explicitly at its centre, social work will become a strong, diverse profession, united in its commitment to common values through a living, debated code of ethics.

In Part Two we examined codes of ethics, particularly the IFSW's *Ethics in Social Work, Statement of Principles* (2004) with its focus on the two principles of human rights and human dignity and social justice, and its commitment to leave detailed regulations up to individual countries' codes of ethics. This statement offers the promise of renewed clarity and direction for social work while allowing space for the inclusion of difference. We argue that if, as a profession, we take up this promise and clarify what we mean by terms such as 'social justice' and 'human rights and dignity', within an holistic understanding that views the individual as part of their social environment, social work will be better placed to recognise when dominant political forces, such as neo-liberalism, attempt to restrict its approach and sphere of activity.

Over the past 40 years or so, due to our lack of clarity and analysis (and thus our acceptance by default of neo-liberal understandings of concepts such as 'human rights' and 'social justice'), social work has largely been ensnared by neo-liberalism and has been mostly silent in the face of the increasing inequality, the ever-widening gap between a growing proportion of disadvantaged people and tiny elites, and shrinking welfare resources available to the poor and disadvantaged. In our silence we have colluded with the attack on morality itself, which views people in need as being 'welfare dependent' instead of seeing that we are all interdependent. Social work instead needs to return to its moral core: the belief that the responsibility to care for each other is one of the most important characteristics that defines our humanity.

Once social work is clear about its telos or purpose, it can refocus on its project of globalisation from below, joining the struggle to address the current imbalance in globalisation by which only the voices and interests of the most powerful are heard. This struggle is carried out at local, national and international levels. Social workers, with their years of experience working with disadvantaged peoples, their goals of social justice and commitment to human rights and dignity, have a wealth of experience, skills and knowledge to offer and a real contribution to make. Already leadership is provided by many individual social workers. With a new commitment to ethical practice, our contribution as a profession can only increase.

When social workers consciously become ethical activists, they can work inclusively, cohesively and collectively towards globalisation from below. They will recognise their worth and be proud of their profession, notwithstanding being in the minority who speak out for an ethical world. One of the main strategies in this struggle is to form alliances with the poor and oppressed and others with the same telos or purpose to promote human flourishing.

In Part Three we discussed three ethical practice issues that confront social workers in their relationships at the client-worker-agency level. First, we argued that the concept of self-determination can help us find a middle road between autonomy and paternalism. Second, we explored how privacy and confidentiality should be delineated and argued that viewing confidentiality as a practice standard that rests on other more fundamental principles will help clarify many practice questions involving confidentiality. Third, we considered the problems involved in the conflict between social control and toleration, and the question of how to balance sincere moral judgement with respect for diversity.

What does this approach to ethical practice mean for the profession?

There are three main issues that social work as a profession has to address, if this approach to ethical practice is to become a reality. First, social work has to acknowledge the centrality of ethics, that social work is in essence an ethical project. This means that all social workers must become ethically articulate and have high levels of ethical virtues, knowledge and skills. It also means that social work has to clarify its understandings of terms such as social justice, so that the discourse of social justice is no longer so easily hijacked by ideologies such as neo-liberalism.

The second issue, which follows from the first, is that ethics must become a central part of social work education around the world, not the peripheral subject it often is today. Teaching ethics needs to have the same importance as teaching social work practice knowledge and skill because it is the heart of social work knowledge and skill. Unless social workers understand and can act upon the ethical dimension to their practice, they will be unable to work coherently towards their goals of social justice and human wellbeing.

The third issue for social work as a profession is the need to develop strong collective networks and organisations, both to support individual social workers in their daily practice and to provide a clear voice for human wellbeing and social justice at local, national and international levels. More focus on social work's collective voice and greater emphasis on working together as a profession will be an important change to enable social work to realise its telos.

What does this approach to ethical practice mean for individual social workers?

With this approach, ethics becomes everyone's business (Hugman 2003). No longer is ethics a matter for experts—it is the heart and soul of a social worker's daily life. Social workers will see themselves as ethical activists, recognising the ethical dimension to the decisions they make every day, consciously using their codes of ethics to help them think through their decisions, and discussing ethical issues with colleagues, supervisors and clients as part of their daily professional responsibility. Becoming ethically articulate will be a central social work characteristic.

To become ethically empowered, social workers will understand the plural nature of ethics and keep in mind the '360-degree assessment cycle' of ethical decision-making, referring to three main ethical modes when making decisions:

- their integrity or professional virtue, and making sure that they are being the sort of person they want to be, including keeping their critical, analytical and reflective senses sharpened;
- their commitment to and knowledge of rules and obligations grounded in respect for human rights and human dignity; and
- their commitment to goals of social justice for all people, the outcomes towards which they are working.

Social workers will accept responsibility and defend their right to make their own ethical decisions, rejecting social pressures to avoid this responsibility through means such as specific procedural formulas or sticking to the letter of the law.

Codes of ethics will be very visible in a world where social workers practice from their ethical base. Codes of ethics will be living documents, referred to, debated and constantly under review.

In their daily practice with individuals, groups, organisations and communities, social workers will be aware of the local, national and global implications of what they are doing. They will understand

that their ability to work with their environments, including organisational policies and processes, is just as important as their ability
to work with clients. They will act much more collectively, contributing to and relying upon a strong professional base from which to
mount their arguments and make a stand. Working collectively means
not only developing professional networks, but also building alliances
and partnerships with groups of disadvantaged people and other
professionals working towards similar goals of social justice and human
rights. Using the ancient notion of classifying people according to their
purpose or telos, it will be easy to identify the people with whom we

Figure 10.1: A conceptual map of ethical practice in social work

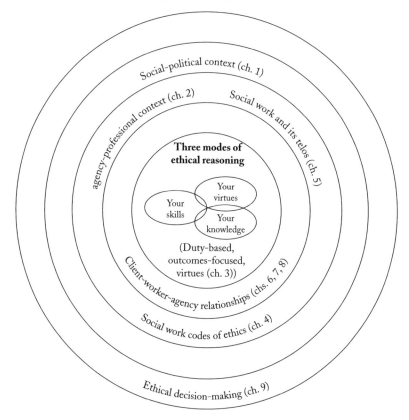

should be working, and to develop more inclusive notions of what we mean by social work.

The three themes: Virtues, ethical skills and ethical knowledge

The virtues, knowledge and skills needed by social workers for ethical practice as discussed in this book are listed below. The following matrix summarises the way we have developed these themes throughout the book. The list is not meant to be exhaustive. Rather it is the beginning of the conversation.

Figure 10.1 offers a conceptual schema of how we see these themes relating to ethical practice. This is a simplified picture designed to show links in the 'big picture' and is not by any means an explanation of the complex relationships the book discusses. The concentric circles show your virtues, ethical skills and knowledge at the centre of ethical practice, surrounded by the three ethical modes or ways of ethical thinking and the 360-degree assessment process that we have discussed. Interacting with these, with 'arrows of influence' going from the centre to each outer ring and coming back in again, are the contexts or environments of social work practice that we have discussed: the issues experienced at the organisation-client-worker level, the issues stemming from the professional/organisational sphere including codes of ethics and organisational processes, and finally the socio-political-ideological environment in which all these other spheres exist.

When thinking about this circle, it is important to remember Payne's (2005) point, that each sphere or arena interacts with and influences the other. Just as the socio-political context influences social work, so can social work influence that context as well as the more immediate ones in which we work. Similarly, the client groups with whom we work in partnership can influence us and our contexts, just as we influence them.

Table 10.1 The development of virtues, ethical skills and ethical knowledge through the book

Chapter/case study	Virtues (cultivate this way of being)	Ethical skills (focus on how to . . .)	Ethical knowledge (understand/ learn this)
1. Socio-political context	Open-mindedness	Critical analysis Informal logic Valid arguments Syllogisms	Teleology
2. Professional context	Practical reasoning	Situational awareness Research/ information seeking Sound argument	Satisficing
3. What is ethics	Moral courage	How to argue Fallacies	Dilemmas/ problems/issues
4. Codes of ethics	Reflectiveness Critical reflection	Communication	Pluralism
5. Telos of social work	Empathy	Self-awareness	Human wellbeing Social justice
6. Autonomy	Integrity Commitment to social work values	Leadership	Respect for persons
7. Privacy	Discretion	Capacity to work collaboratively	Rights
8. Toleration	Tolerance Valuing diversity	Ethical activism	Cultural relativism
9. Ethical decision-making	Good judgement, 'wisdom'	Scepticism 360-degree assessments	Thought experiments Counter factuals

Conclusion

Notwithstanding the complexities of power in our postmodern global-ised world, discussed in chapter 1, ethics can empower social work. Ethical social work practice is about social workers becoming ethical activists. This means acting ethically in professional contexts, and actively challenging and working to change those contexts if they do not support human wellbeing. With ethics as its driving force, social work can be a diverse profession, united in its commitment to common values through a living, debated, code of ethics.

This is not an easy road. In our current postmodern world domi-nated by neo-liberalism, social work joins a minority of voices arguing for an ethical approach. In the words of Zygmunt Bauman (2000) to new social workers:

> I cannot promise a quiet night's sleep, a quiet conscience, or feeling comfortable . . . The decision to be a social worker means a very rewarding, satisfying and extremely difficult life.

References

Adams, R., Dominelli, L. and Payne, M. (eds) 2002, *Critical Practice in Social Work*, Palgrave, Basingstoke.

Agger, B. 1992, *The Discourses of Domination*, Northwestern University Press, Evanston.

Alexandra, A., Matthews, S. and Miller, S. 2002, *Reasons, Values and Institutions*, Tertiary Press, Croydon.

Allen, J., Pease, B. and Briskman, L. (eds) 2003, *Critical Social Work*, Allen & Unwin, Sydney.

Alston, M. and McKinnon, J. 2001, 'Introduction', in M. Alston and J. McKinnon (eds), *Social Work Fields of Practice*, Oxford University Press, South Melbourne, pp. xv–xxxiv.

Alston, M. and McKinnon, J. (eds) 2005, *Social Work Fields of Practice* (2nd edn), Oxford University Press, South Melbourne.

Amnesty International <http://www.amnesty.org/ailib/intcam/femgen/fgm1.htm/>.

Aotearoa New Zealand Association of Social Workers (ANZASW) 1993, *Code of Ethics*, Dunedin, New Zealand.

Aristotle 2002, *Nicomachean Ethics*, translated and edited by Christopher Rowe, Oxford University Press, Oxford.

Australian Association of Social Workers (AASW) 2000, *AASW Code of Ethics*, Australian Association of Social Workers, Barton, ACT.

Banks, S. 1995, *Ethics and Values in Social Work*, Macmillan, London.

Banks, S. 1998, 'Professional Ethics in Social Work—What future?', *British Journal of Social Work*, vol. 28, pp. 213–31.

Banks, S. 2001, *Ethics and Values in Social Work* (2nd edn), Palgrave Macmillan, Basingstoke, Hampshire.

Banks, S. 2002, 'Professional Values and Accountabilities', in R. Adams, L. Dominelli and M. Payne (eds), *Critical Practice in Social Work*, Palgrave, Basingstoke, Hampshire, pp. 28–37.

Banks, S. 2004, *Ethics, Accountability and the Social Professions*, Palgrave Macmillan, Basingstoke.

Banks, S. and Williams, R. 2005, 'Accounting for Ethical Difficulties in Social Welfare Work: Issues, problems and dilemmas', *British Journal of Social Work*, vol. 35, no. 7, pp. 1005–22.

Barry, B. 1989, *Theories of Justice*, Harvester-Wheatsheaf, London.

Bauman, Z. 1993, *Postmodern Ethics*, Blackwell, Oxford.

Bauman, Z. 1995, *Life in Fragments: Essays in Postmodern Morality*, Blackwell, Oxford.

Bauman, Z. 2000, *A Meeting with Zygmunt Bauman* (Video), Oslo University College, Norway.

Beauchamp and Childress 1989, *Principles of Biomedical Ethics* (4th edn), Oxford University Press, Oxford and New York.

Benn, S. 1988, *A Theory of Freedom*, Cambridge University Press, Cambridge.

Bellamy, R. 1992, *Liberalism and Modern Society*, Polity, Cambridge.

Biestek, F. 1961, *The Casework Relationship*, Allen & Unwin, London.

Bisman, C. 2004, 'Social Work Values: The moral core of the profession', *British Journal of Social Work*, vol. 34, no. 1, pp. 109–23.

Bok, S. 1984, *Secrets: On the ethics of concealment and revelation*, Oxford University Press, New York.

Bowring, W. 2002, 'Forbidden Relations? The UK's Discourse of Human Rights and the Struggle for Social Justice', *Social Justice and Global Development Journal (LGD)* 2002(1) <http>//www2. warwick.ac.uk/fac/soc/law/elj/lgd/220_1/bowring/>.

Brecher, J., Costello, T. and Smith, B. 2002, 'Globalization and its Specter' in *Globalization from Below: The power of solidarity* (2nd edn), South End Press, Cambridge, Massachusetts, pp. 1–17.

Briskman, L. and Noble, C. 1999, 'Social Work Ethics: Embracing diversity?', in B. Pease and J. Fook (eds), *Transforming Social Work Practice: Postmodern critical perspectives*, Allen & Unwin, Sydney, pp. 57–69.

British Association of Social Workers (BASW) 2002, 'The Code of Ethics for Social Work', <http://www.basw.co.uk/pages/info/ethics. htm>.

Bush, M. 1996, A Report to the Australian Association of Social Workers Ltd New South Wales Branch Ethics Committee on Inquiries to AASW (NSW) Branch Ethics Committee 1986–1993, AAWS NSW Branch, Sydney, September.

Butrym, Z. 1976, *The Nature of Social Work*, Macmillan, London.

Calvez, J. and Perrin, J. 1961, *The Church and Social Justice: The teaching of the Popes from Leo XIII to Pius XII, 1878–1958*, J. Kirwan (trans.), Henry Regenry, Chicago.

Canadian Association of Social Workers (CASW) 2005, Homepage <http://www.casw-acts.ca/>.

Chenoweth, L. and McAuliffe, D. 2005, *The Road to Social Work and Human Service Practice: An introductory text*, Thomson, Victoria.

Clark, C.L. 2000, *Social Work Ethics, Politics, Principles and Practice*, Macmillan, London.

Clark, C.L. and Asquith, S. 1985, *Social Work and Social Philosophy: A guide to practice*, Routledge and Kegan Paul, London.

Clarke, J. and Newman, J. 1997, *The Managerial State*, Sage, London.

Coady, M. and Bloch, S. (eds) 1996, C*odes of Ethics and the Professions*, Melbourne University Press, Melbourne.

Cohen, S. 2004, *The Nature of Moral Reasoning*, Oxford University Press, South Melbourne.

Collingridge, M. 1991, 'Legal Risk, Legal Scrutiny, and Social Workers', *Australian Social Work*, vol. 44, no. 1, pp. 11–17.

Collingridge, M. 1995, 'Social Service Work and Ethical Codes', in S. Miller (ed.), *Professional Ethics*, Keon Publications, Wagga Wagga, pp. 64–77.

Collingridge, M., Miller, S. and Bowles, W. 2001, 'Privacy and Confidentiality in Social Work', *Australian Social Work*, vol. 54, no. 2, pp. 3–13.

Considine, M. 1994, *Public Policy: A critical approach*, Macmillan Education Australia, Melbourne.

Cossins, A. and Pilkington, R. 1996, 'Balancing the Scales: The case for the inadmissability of counselling records in sexual assault trials', *UNSW Law Journal*, vol. 19, no. 1, pp. 222–67.

Cottone, R.R. 2001, 'A Social Constructivism Model of Ethical Decison-making in Counselling', *Journal of Counseling and Development*, vol. 79, pp. 39–45.

Cottone, R.R. and Claus, R.E. 2000, 'Ethical Decision-making Models: A review of the literature', *Journal of Counseling and Development*, vol. 78, no. 3, pp. 275–83.

Craig, G. 2002, 'Poverty, Social Work and Social Justice', *British Journal of Social Work*, vol. 32, no. 6, pp. 669–82.

Davis, A.H. 1997, 'The Ethics of Caring: A collaborative approach to resolving ethical dilemmas', *Journal of Applied Rehabilitation Counselling*, vol. 28, no. 1, pp. 36–41.

Deakin, N. 1999, 'The Management of Welfare', in H. Weber (ed.), *The Future of the Welfare State: British and German Perspectives*, Trier, Wissenschaftlicher Verlag Trier, pp. 178–86.

Del Vecchio, G. 1952, *Justice: An historical and philosophical essay* (English edn), Edinburgh University Press, Edinburgh.

De Maria, W. 1997, 'Flapping on Clipped Wings: Social work ethics in the age of activism', *Australian Social Work*, vol. 50, no. 4, pp. 3–19.

Descartes, R. 2003, *Discourse on Methods and Meditations*, E.S. Haldane and G.R.T. Ross (trans.), Dover Publications, Mineola, New York.

Dominelli, L. 2002, 'Values in Social Work: Contested entities with enduring qualities', in R. Adams, L. Dominelli and M. Payne (eds), *Critical Practice in Social Work*, Palgrave, Basingstoke, pp. 15–27.

Donovan, E. and Jackson, A. 1991, *Managing Human Service Organisations*, Prentice Hall, Sydney.

Dworkin, G. 2002, 'Paternalism', in *The Standford Encyclopaedia of Philosophy*, E. Zalta (ed.), Winter 2002, <http:/plato.standford.edu/archives/win2002/entries/paternalism>.

Dworkin, R. 1977, *Taking Rights Seriously*, Duckworth, London.

Etzioni, A. (ed.) 1969, *The Semi-Professions and the Organization*, Free Press, New York.

Etzioni, A. 1999, *The Limits of Privacy*, Basic Books, New York.

Finn, P. 1992, 'Professionals and Confidentiality', *Sydney Law Review*, vol. 14, pp. 317–39.

Fook, J. 1999, 'Critical Reflexivity in Education and Practice', in B. Pease and J. Fook (eds), *Social Work Practice*, Allen & Unwin, Sydney.

Fook, J. 2002, *Social Work Critical Theory and Practice*, Sage, London; Thousand Oaks, New Delhi.

Forester-Miller, H. and Davis, T.E. 1995, *A Practitioner's Guide to Ethical Decision Making*, American Counseling Association, Alexandria, Virginia.

Foucault, M. 1972, *The Archaeology of Knowledge*, A.M. Sheridan Smith (trans.), Pantheon Books, New York.

Foucault, M. 1977, *Discipline and Punish*, A.M. Sheridan Smith (trans.), Pantheon Books, New York.

Freeman, S.J. 2000, *Ethics: An Introduction to Philosophy and Practice*, Wadsworth/Thomson, Belmont.

Freud, S. and Krug, S. 2002, 'Beyond the Code of Ethics, Part I: Complexities of ethical decision making in social work practice', *Families in Society*, vol. 83, no. 5/6, pp. 474–82.

Fried, C. 1968, 'Privacy', *Yale Law Journal*, vol. 77, p. 474.

Garcia, J.G., Cartwright, B., Winston, S.M. and Borzuchowska, B. 2003, 'A Transcultural Integrative Model for Ethical Decision-making in Counselling', *Journal of Counseling and Development*, vol. 81, no. 3.

Gardner, F. 2006, *Working with Human Service Organisations—Creating connections for practice*, Oxford University Press, Victoria.

Gray, J. 1995, *Liberalism* (2nd edn), University of Minnesota Press, Minneapolis.

Gray, M. 1995, 'The Ethical Implications of Current Theoretical Developments in Social Work', *British Journal of Social Work*, vol. 25, pp. 55–70.

Gray, P. 1991, *Psychology*, Worth Publishers Inc., New York.

Greif, G.L. 2004, 'When a Social Worker Becomes a Voluntary Commissioner and Calls on the Code of Ethics', *Social Work*, vol. 49, no. 2, pp. 277–80.

Harries, M. 1996, 'Ethics, the law and professional practice for South Australian Branch Ethics Committee', paper presented to South Australian Branch of Australian Association of Social Workers, July.

Healy, K. 2004, 'Social Workers in the New Human Services Marketplace: Trends, challenges and responses', *Australian Social Work*, vol. 57, no. 2, pp. 103–14.

Healy, K. 2005, *Social Work Theories in Context: Creating frameworks for practice*, Palgrave Macmillan, Houndmills, Basingstoke, Hampshire, New York.

Herodotus 2003, *The Histories*, translated by Aubrey de Selincourt, edited by J. Marincola, Penguin, Harmondsworth.

Heywood, A. 2000, *Key Concepts in Politics*, Macmillan, Houndmills.

Hill, M. 1997, *The Policy Process in the Modern State* (3rd edn), Prentice Hall, Hertfordshire.

Hirschman, A.O. 1970, *Exit Voice and Loyalty: Responses to decline in firms, organisations, and states*, Harvard University Press, Cambridge, Massachusetts.

Holland, T.P. and Kilpatrick, A.C. 1991, 'Ethical Issues in Social Work: Towards a grounded theory of professional ethics', *Social Work*, vol. 36, no. 2, pp. 138–44.

Hollis, M. and Howe, D. 1987, 'Moral Risks in Social Work', *Journal of Applied Philosophy*, vol. 4, pp. 123–33.

Hugman, R. 2003, 'Professional Ethics in Social Work: Living with the legacy', *Australian Social Work*, vol. 56, no. 1, pp. 5–15.

Hugman, R. 2005, *New Approaches in Ethics for the Caring Professions*, Palgrave Macmillan, Houndmills, Basingstoke, Hampshire, New York.

Hugman, R. and Smith, D. (eds) 1995, *Ethical Issues in Social Work*, Routledge, London.

Hursthouse, R. 1999 *On Virtue Ethics*, Oxford University Press, New York.

Husserl, E. 1931, *Ideas: General Introduction to Pure Phenomenology*, W.R. Boyce Gibson (trans.), George Allen & Unwin, London.

Ife, J. 1997, *Rethinking Social Work: Towards a critical practice*, Longman, South Melbourne.

Ife, J. 2000, 'Community-based Options for Social Work: Sites for creative practice', in I. O'Connor, P. Smyth and J. Warburton (eds), *Contemporary Perspectives on Social Work and the Human Services: Challenges and change*, Longman, Sydney.

Ife, J. 2001, *Human Rights and Social Work: Towards rights-based practice*, Cambridge University Press, Cambridge.

Ife, J. 2002, *Community Development: Community-based alternatives in an age of globalisation* (2nd edn), Longman, Sydney.

International Federation of Social Workers (IFSW) 2002, *Definition of Social Work*, <http://ifsw.org/Publications>.

International Federation of Social Workers (IFSW) 2004, *Ethics in Social Work, Statement of Principles*, <http://ifsw.org/en/p3800324. htm>.

Internet Encyclopedia of Philosophy, <http://www.iep.utm.edu/f/ fallacies.htm>.

Jones, A. and May, J. 1992, *Working in Human Service Organisations: A critical introduction*, Longman Cheshire, Melbourne.

Keeley, M. and Graham J.W. 1991, 'Exit, Voice, and Ethics', *Journal of Business Ethics*, vol. 10, pp. 350–1.

Kerr, L. and Savelsberg, H. 2001, 'Unemployment and civic responsibility in Australia: Towards a new social contract', *Critical Social Policy*, vol. 19, no. 2.

Khinduka, S. 2004, 'Globalisation and Social Work: Challenges and possibilities', invited lecture to social work students, Charles Sturt University, September.

Koehn, D., 1994, *The Ground of Professional Ethics*, Routledge, New York.

Kultgen, J. 1988, *Ethics and Professionalism*, University of Pennsylvania Press, Philadelphia.

Leach, R. 1993, *Political Ideologies* (2nd edn), Macmillan, Melbourne.

McArdle, J. 1998, *Resource Manual for Facilitators in Community Development*, vol. 2, Vista, Melbourne.

McBeath, G. and Webb, S.A. 2002, 'Virtue Ethics and Social Work: Being lucky, realistic, and not doing one's duty', *British Journal of Social Work*, vol. 32, pp. 1015–36.

March, J.G. and Simon, H.A. 1958, *Organizations*, Wiley, New York.

Metherell, M. and Gauntlett, K. 2004, 'Fuel for Hygiene—Aborigines strike deal', *Sydney Morning Herald*, 9 December, p. 1.

Mill, J.S. (1859) 1987, *On Liberty*, Penguin, Harmondsworth.

Minor, M. and Petocz, A. 2003, 'Moral Theory in Ethical Decision Making: Problems, clarifications and recommendations from a psychological perspective', *Journal of Business Ethics*, vol. 42, no. 1.

Morris, P.M. 2002, 'The Capabilities Perspective: A framework for social justice', *Families in Society*, vol. 83, no. 4, pp. 365–73.

Mouzelis, N. 1975, *Organizations and Bureaucracy* (2nd edn), Routledge and Kegan Paul, London.

Mullaly, R.P. 1997, *Structural Social Work: Ideology, theory, and practice* (2nd edn), Oxford University Press, Toronto.

Nabben, R. 2001, 'Managerialism, the "quality movement" and community services—Dancing with the devil?', *Just Policy*, no. 22, June, pp. 43–7.

National Association of Social Workers (NASW) 1999, *Code of Ethics of the National Association of Social Workers*, <http://www. socialwork-ers.org/pubs/code/code.asp>.

Neave, M. 1987, 'Confidentiality and the Duty to Warn', *University of Tasmania Law Review*, vol. 9, pp. 1–31.

Noble, C. and Briskman, L. 1998, 'Workable Ethics: Social work and progressive practice', *Australian Social Work*, vol. 51, no. 3, pp. 9–15.

Noyoo, N. 2004, 'Human Rights and Social Work in a Transforming Society: South Africa', *International Social Work*, vol. 47, no. 3, pp. 359–69.

NSW Law Handbook 2005, Redfern Legal Centre Publishing, Sydney.

Oakley, J. and Cocking, D. 2001, *Virtue Ethics and Professional Roles*, Cambridge University Press, Cambridge.

Office of the Federal Privacy Commissioner (Australia), <http://www. privacy.gov.au/>.

Office of the Privacy Commissioner (New Zealand), <http://www. privacy.org.nz/>.

Pakulski, J. 2004, *Globalising Inequalities: New patterns of social privilege and disadvantage*, Allen & Unwin, Sydney.

Parton, N. and Byrne, P. 2000, *Constructive Social Work: Towards a new practice*, Palgrave, Basingstoke.

Parton, N., Thorpe, D. and Wattam, C. 1997, *Child Protection, Risk and the Moral Order*, MacMillan, Basingstoke.

Pawar, M. 1999, 'Australian and Indian Social Work Codes of Ethics', *Australian Journal of Professional and Applied Ethics*, vol. 2, no. 2, pp. 72–85.

Payne, M. 2005, *Modern Social Work Theory* (3rd edn), Palgrave Macmillan, Houndmills, Basingstoke, Hampshire, New York.

Perry, R. 1993, 'Empathy—Still at the Heart of Therapy: The interplay of context and empathy', *The Australian and New Zealand Journal of Family Therapy*, vol. 14, no. 2, pp. 63–74.

Pinkerton, J. and Campbell, J. 2002, 'Social Work and Social Justice in Northern Ireland: Towards a new occupational space', *British Journal of Social Work*, vol. 32, no. 6, pp. 723–37.

Polack, R. 2004, 'Social Justice and the Global Economy: New challenges for social work in the 21st century', *Social Work*, vol. 49, no. 2, pp. 281–90.

Pollitt, C. 1990, *Managerialism and the Public Services*, Blackwell, Oxford.

Powell, F. 2001, *The Politics of Social Work*, Sage, London.

Pusey, M. 1991, *Economic Rationalism in Canberra*, Press Syndicate University of Cambridge, Cambridge.

Rachels, J. 2003, *The Elements of Moral Philosophy* (4th edn), McGraw-Hill, New York.

Rathbone-McCuan, E. and Fabian, D.R. 1992, *Self-neglecting Elders: A clinical dilemma*, Auburn House, New York.

Rawls, J. 1971, *A Theory of Justice*, Belknap Press, Massachusetts.

Rawls, J. 1996, *Political Liberalism*, Columbia University Press, New York.

Raz, J. 1986, *The Morality of Freedom*, Clarendon, Oxford.

Reamer, F. 2001, *Social Work Values and Ethics*, Columbia, New York.

Reichert, E. 2003, *Social Work and Human Rights: A foundation for policy and practice*, Columbia University Press, New York.

Rhodes, M. 1986, *Ethical Dilemmas in Social Work Practice*, Routledge and Kegan Paul, Boston.

Robertson, C.J. and Crittendon, W.F. 2003, 'Mapping Moral Philosophies: Strategic implications for multinational firms', *Strategic Management Journal*, vol. 24, no. 4, pp. 385–92.

Rooney, R. 1992, *Strategies for Work with Involuntary Clients*, Columbia University Press, New York.

Saleebey, D. (ed.) 2002, *The Strengths Perspective in Social Work Practice*, Allyn and Bacon, Boston, Massachusetts.

Scanlon, E. and Longres, F.J. 2001, 'Social Justice and Social Work: A reply to Leroy Pelton', *Journal of Social Work Education*, vol. 37, no. 3, pp. 441–4.

Sen, A. 1985, *Commodities and Capabilities*, Elsevier, Amsterdam.

Sevenhuijsen, S. 1998, *Citizenship and the Ethics of Care: Feminist considerations on justice, morality and politics*, Routledge, New York.

Sidanius, J. and Pratto, F. 1999, *Social Dominance: An intergroup theory of social hierarchy and oppression*, Cambridge University Press, Cambridge.

Simon, H.A. 1976, *Administrative Behavior: A study of decision-making processes in administrative organizations* (first published in 1945), Free Press, New York.

Sinclair, A. 1996, 'Codes in the Workplace: Organisational versus professional codes', in M. Coady and S. Bloch (eds), *Codes of Ethics and the Professions*, Melbourne University Press, Melbourne, pp. 88–108.

Social Work Educators' Forum 1997, 'Declaration of Ethics for Professional Social Workers', *The Indian Journal of Social Work*, vol. 58, no. 2, pp. 335–41.

Stanford Encyclopedia of Philosophy, <http://plato.stanford.edu/>.

Sullivan, W.M. 2004, *Work and Integrity: The Crisis and Promise of Professionalism in America*, Jossey-Bass, San Francisco, California.

Swanton, C. 2001, 'Virtue Ethical Account of Rights Action', *Ethics*, vol. 112, no. 1, pp. 32–43.

Tabb, W.K. 2001, *The Amoral Elephant*, Monthly Review Press, New York.

Tarvydas, V.M. 1998, 'Ethical Decision-making Processes', in R.R. Cottone and V.M. Tarvydas (eds), *Ethical and Professional Issues in Counselling*, Prentice Hall, New Jersey, pp. 144–54.

Taylor, C. 1986, 'The Nature and Scope of Distributive Justice', in F. Lucash (ed.), *Justice and Equality Here and Now*, Cornell University Press, London.

Thompson, N. 2002, 'Social Movements, Social Justice and Social Work', *British Journal of Social Work*, vol. 32, no. 6, pp. 711–22.

Tredennick, H. 1969, 'Ethics, Character and Authentic Transformational Leadership', *Leadership Quarterly*, vol. 10, no. 2, pp. 181–218.

United Nations: Human Rights website, <http://www.un.org/rights/>.

Valentine, B. 2005, 'An Exploration of the Constructs of Social Justice in the Australian Social Work Discourse', Unpublished PhD thesis, Charles Sturt University, Wagga Wagga.

van Berkel, R. and Moller, I. 2002, 'Introduction', in R. van Berkel and I. Moller (eds), *Active Social Policies in the EU*, Policy Press, Bristol.

van den Broek, D. 2003, 'Selling Human Services: Public sector, rationalisation and the call centre labour process', *Australian Bulletin of Labour*, vol. 29, no. 3, September, pp. 236–52.

Waligorski, C. 1997, *Liberal Economics and Democracy*, University Press of Kansas, Kansas.

Warren, S.D. and Brandeis, L.D. 1890, 'The Right to Privacy', *Harvard Law Review*, p. 4.

Watson, D. and Leighton, N. 1985, 'What's the Point of a Code of Ethics for Social Work?', in D. Watson (ed.), *A Code of Ethics for Social Work: The second step*, Routledge and Kegan Paul, London.

Weber, M. 1983, *Max Weber on Capitalism, Bureaucracy, and Religion: A selection of texts*, Stanislav Andreski (ed.), Allen & Unwin, London.

Welfel, E.R. 2002, *Ethics in Counselling and Psychotherapy: Standards, research and emerging issues* (2nd edn), Brooks/Cole Thompson, Pacific Grove, California.

Westin, A.F. 1967, *Privacy and Freedom*, Antheum, New York.

Wicclair, M.R. 1993, *Ethics and the Elderly*, Oxford University Press, New York.

Wilson, S. 1978, *Confidentiality in Social Work*, Free Press, New York.

Wissenburg, M. 1999, *Imperfection and Impartiality*, UCL Press, London.

Wood, C. 1997, 'To Know or Not to Know: A critique of postmodernism in social work practice', *Australian Social Work*, vol. 50, no. 3, pp. 21–7.

Yeatman, A. (ed.) 1998, *Activism and the Policy Process*, Allen & Unwin, Sydney.

Young, I. 1990, *Justice and the Politics of Difference*, Princeton University Press, Princeton, New Jersey.

Younghusband, E. 1970, 'Social Work and Social Values', *Social Work Today*, vol. 1, no. 6.

Index